Graphic Communications for the Performing Arts

Graphic Communications for

the Performing Arts

David J. Skal, editor

Robert E. Callahan, designer

Published by

TheatreCommunications
Group, Inc.

with the support of the
National Endowment for the Arts,
Design Arts Program

1981

About TCG

Theatre Communications Group, Inc. is the national service organization for the nonprofit professional theatre. Founded in 1961, TCG provides more than 25 artistic, administrative and informational services to a constituency of nearly 200 resident, experimental, ethnic and other nonprofit professional theatres located throughout the United States, as well as to independent theatre artists, technicians and administrators. TCG provides a forum for the profession and a resource for the media, funding agencies and the public.

TCG is supported by the Alcoa Foundation, the Robert Sterling Clark Foundation, the William H. Donner Foundation, Equitable Life Assurance Society of the United States, Exxon Corporation, the Ford Foundation, the William and Flora Hewlett Foundation, the Andrew W. Mellon Foundation, the National Endowment for the Arts, the New York Community Trust, the New York State Council on the Arts and the Scherman Foundation.

Typography by Blue Pen Typografix, Inc., New York City
Printed by the Press of A. Colish, Mount Vernon, New York
Library of Congress Catalogue Number 81-51181
ISBN 0-930452-11-9
$12.95

Acknowledgements

The photographs on pages 32-35 appear through the courtesy of Daniel C. Gerould and Alma H. Law, from the catalogue of the exhibition, *Polish and Soviet Theatre Posters,* held at the Graduate Center of the City University of New York, June 30–September 15, 1980, under the auspices of the Center for Advanced Study in Theatre Arts (CASTA) with support from the National Endowment for the Humanities.

In addition to the institutions and designers represented, the editor wishes to thank the following individuals for their support, advice and special assistance during the compilation of this volume: Mark Arnold, Kirsten Beck, Elaine Binno, Richard Bryant, Samuel R. Crowl, Doug Eichten, Richard Frankel, Margaret Glover, Laurie Hughes, Caryn Katkin, Nosrat Khansari, Kathleen Johnston, Charles Judge, Stuart Leventhal, Rosalie Lewis, Ted Malter, Paul Pierson, P.J. Prokop, Hilary Roberts-Dasculi, Selma Rudnick, Amy Schlosser, Liz Skrodski, Richard Sprague, Deborah J. Weiner, Van Westover, Suellen Wolfson, Peter Zeisler, Lindy Zesch and Ron Zins.

Special thanks to Alan Krauss for his diligent and perceptive copyediting and proofreading.

DJS

Contents

Introduction

While the performing arts in America have historically placed a great emphasis on visual achievement on stage, relatively small attention has been paid to the visual quality of the printed communications upon which their very existence depends. Performing arts organizations rely heavily—and sometimes exclusively—on printed materials for selling tickets, soliciting donations and generally informing the public about their unique identities. Regrettably, due in part to budgetary constraints, the performing arts have frequently neglected design quality in this vital area.

Recent years, however, have seen a perceptible shift toward good design systems, enough to fill an entire book with outstanding examples of graphic design for the performing arts, almost all of which have been achieved in a nonprofit context. *Graphic Communications for the Performing Arts* intends to demonstrate how good design can be integral to an organization's artistic, managerial and marketing activities. It is intended for use by arts administrators, marketing specialists, graphic designers, advertising agencies, art students—in short, anyone whose work involves or will involve printed communications for the arts.

The question inevitably arises: just what *is* good design? And, inevitably, there is no simple answer. Visual communications, after all, are concerned more with ways of seeing rather than ways of theorizing. But there are certain attributes and attitudes that successful design projects seem to share, and which are worthy of discussion.

To begin with, good design is good communication. That is to say, good design springs naturally from a well-organized message, which it transmits expressively without undue distraction or interference. Good design usually involves focus and simplification rather than embellishment. It may be bold or subtle, pictorial or typographical, colorful or monochromatic, or a combinaton of all these things (there is a common and unfortunate tendency these days to equate "good design" with stark expanses of white space and austere sans-serif typefaces). Whatever its components, good design commands attention, conveys credibility and transmits information in a heightened, presentational form.

Properly utilized, good design is also good business. It obviously makes good business sense for an arts organization (or any other group) to carefully coordinate the appearance of its printed materials. A firmly established "image" in print requires far less reinforcement (i.e., promotional expenditure) than a constantly shifting or weakly established graphic identity. Continuity of public awareness is particularly important to performing arts organizations, dependent as they are on subscription sales and repeated business.

For all its virtues, however, good design should not be confused with good *marketing*. Design coordination is certainly a basic principle in modern marketing, but good design *per se* will not sell tickets, solve your management problems, or raise the funds needed to build your new symphony hall. To be perfectly honest, badly designed materials can be used quite effectively to sell

1

New York City Ballet
Poster
Designer: Donn Matus
Photographer: Martha Swope
Dancer: Patricia McBride

subscriptions and raise money—if they're utilized energetically within a solid marketing concept.

No, good design is not always "necessary." But, by the same line of reasoning, neither are the performing arts "necessary."

Which brings us to perhaps our most important consideration. Beyond the obvious utilitarian and promotional advantages of good design, there is yet another reason for arts organizations to strive for graphic excellence. Among the major functions of the arts have been the creation of order from disorder, the uncovering of patterns, and the achievement of expressive elegance. In an age of relentless media bombardment and communicative clutter, cultural organizations are in a unique position to foster good design and design awareness in society at large. The federal government has been systematically encouraging design excellence throughout its agencies for nearly a decade; certainly the time has come for our institutions most closely involved with aesthetic concerns to take a similar initiative.

This book represents the first for-mal attempt to foster such a development, collecting between two covers the entire spectrum of graphic design as it impacts on the world of nonprofit performance art. Selected examples from the commercial sector and abroad are included for purposes of comparison, and communications specialists from all fields have contributed valuable insights and a diversity of perspectives.

Personally speaking, in the half-dozen years I have been professionally involved in communications for the arts, I have always wanted a single resource to replace the haphazard collection of brochures, posters and other materials that constitute a "reference library" for most arts institutions. To be sure, there were several extant volumes on the history of posters, and a glut of advertising agency annuals, but none of these addressed in a comprehensive way the *specific* needs and concerns of the creative director in a nonprofit cultural institution. If the book were to exist, I realized, it would have to be created. And it was only appropriate that such a book be published by Theatre Communications Group, to complement *Subscribe Now!*, Danny Newman's excellent interdisciplinary volume on audience development and marketing systems.

Here then—following countless hundreds of phone calls, letters and inquiries, several thousand individual submissions, seemingly endless production, printing and design consultations, and (most important) boundless encouragement and support from the field—is that book.

If it does its job, the sequel ought to be fantastic.

David J. Skal
June, 1981

1

2

1
The Feld Ballet
Logo
Designer: Gerry Gentile
Photographer: Bert Stern

2
Toronto Symphony
Poster
Designer/illustrator: Roger Hill

3
Alvin Ailey American Dance Theater
Logo
Designer: William Hampton

3

Institutional Design

The notion of "institutional" or "corporate" identity may strike some as inappropriate to a discussion of the creative arts, bringing to mind images of bureaucratic alienation in a faceless, conglomeratized world. In reality, the concept of corporate identity is as old as commerce itself, with its earliest variations to be found in potters' marks of antiquity. The first trademarks served purposes that continue to this day; they identified a certain kind of product with a particular craftsman or group of craftspeople, protecting their commercial interests and insuring their public recognition.

While the media upon which trademarks are imprinted have evolved from clay to paper to electronically encoded microwaves, the institutional symbol, like the signature, is firmly embedded in the fabric of society and trade. Such symbols are also power symbols—witness the authority invested over the ages in signet rings and royal seals—and are bound inextricably with standing, prestige, credibility, quality, longevity, continuity and so on.

Throughout most of their history, the performing arts have not had to deal much with the problem of an "identity" beyond the time and space of performance. Performances usually took place in places of natural public congregation. It was only the advent of the industrial revolution, with urban sprawl and arbitrary "zoning" of city life, that made it necessary for people to travel significant distances to encounter the performing arts—or to engage in virtually any other activity. The primary encounter of performer with audience and resulting word-of-mouth were no longer sufficient; secondary means— posters, playbills, heralds—became necessary mediators.

The growth of resident performing arts institutions in the United States has also intensified the need for ongoing public awareness of theatre, dance and music as continuing expressions (or products, if you will) of a particular producing organization. The existence of these companies depends literally on this awareness; modern performing arts groups are predicated on subscription audiences— patrons who will, in essence, purchase a *trademark* on faith.

Thus, trademark symbolism enters into a symbiotic partnership with art—the success of one reinforces the other. The best performing groups make the most of this relationship—onstage success encourages public favor; this energy in turn can be channeled into potent words and images which reinforce the primary experience, which encourage greater attendance, and so on.

However, the partnership does entail shared responsibilities. Difficulties can ensue when the reality of the work on stage, for whatever reason, no longer supports the public image. Contrary to mythology, the most sophisticated public relations and advertising cannot "sell" repeated miscalculations on the part of a performing arts group, be they miscalculations of art or simply of the size and sort of audience being sought. Unlike films, touring troupes and circus companies, a *resident* arts organization has to live with the fallout resulting from any perceived dissonance between art and image. It's obviously not wise, in the long run, for a theatre company specializing in Pinter and Ionesco to

1

Tulsa Opera
Embossed letterhead (detail)
Logo designer: Jim Davies
Letterhead designer: Harold Tackett
Agency: Hinkle-Crawford-Davies

"package" itself as a rollicking dinner theatre. The short-term box office benefits will inevitably be just that—short term. A theatre that doesn't want be thought of as a "star barn" should probably avoid graphics that over-emphasize occasional "name" performers.

Graphic imagery is powerful stuff. The ancients recognized the potential of visual symbols as both conceptual tools and vehicles for transformation. We should not forget that all through history people and groups of people have tended to become the images they have projected. The earliest religious (i.e., theatrical) rituals were inextricably bound to symbolic imagery; whether or not we choose to recognize it, this theatre/image/ritual connection is still present on a subliminal level when we talk about graphic images for the performing arts.

Metaphysics aside, there are more than sufficient reasons on a practical plane for maintaining a coherent graphic identity: if graphic imagery has the power to control and shape civilizations, then it certainly has the ability to enhance the day-to-day activities of a theatre company or dance troupe. And the impact of a graphic design system is by no means completely *external* to the organization; there is inevitably a strengthening of *internal* identity that occurs when artists and workers see their goals and activities visually acknowledged in a poster, letterhead or publication. We are all terrifically susceptible to anything that appears "in print"—the mere act of setting type is a ritual that imparts an astonishing charge of credibility and legitimacy.

This chapter is intended to provide an overview of the many interrelated elements of institutional identity in the arts and the ways in which the graphic designer can enhance an organization's image while complementing its unique creative energies.

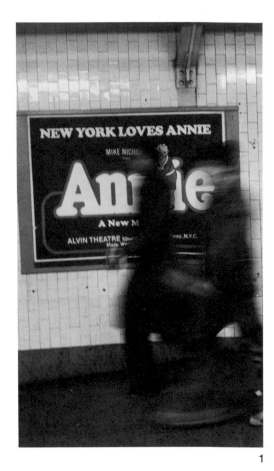

1

1,3,4,5
Commercial theatre graphics
Photographer: Alan Krauss

2
Playwrights Horizons
Sign execution: Christopher Hacker

6
Circle Repertory Company
Banner designer: Chuck Dorris

7
Soho Repertory Theatre
Logo designer: David Uozumi
Building facade and sign: Jerry Engelbach

2

3

5

4

6

7

A good identity system requires *consistent* application; for a performing arts institution, this concept entails all the usual business applications (letterheads, building signage) and the uses which are particular to the performing arts—playbills, posters, opening night invitations, advertising, etc.

These examples of design projects from the Goodman Theatre in Chicago demonstrate the wide range of circumstances in which a theatre can utilize its graphic identity.

1

2

3

4

5

Goodman Theatre

1
_____
Playbill cover
Designer: James McCaffrey
Logo treatment: David Dumo
Creative Director: Eric Hamburger
Agency: The Hagen Group, Inc.

2
_____
Logo
Design: Foote, Cone, and Belding, Inc.

3
_____
Building marquee
Design consultants:
Skidmore, Owings and Merrill,
Architects and Engineers

4
_____
Annual report
Design: Foote, Cone, and Belding, Inc.
Logo treatment: David Dumo

5
_____
Playbill cover
Designer: David Dumo

There are three basic visual elements in an institutional identity system: first, the institutional *symbol,* second the institutional *logotype* or *logo,* (the typographical treatment of the company's name), and finally, the institutional *signature,* which is the characteristic manner in which symbol and logotype are used together for reproduction. Often, logo and symbol are combined as one design or trademark.

The challenge in developing logotypes and symbols for the performing arts is to create designs that are economical, recognizable, and consistent with the inherent *theatricality* of the particular art form.

The designs shown here provide good examples of the varied approaches possible. Perhaps the first institutional theatre logo was the design below for The Guthrie Theater in Minneapolis. With its large signature letter embellished with a heraldic banner, it immediately evokes the kind of classical fanfare for which the company is known. The Tulsa Opera's lavish calligraphy is a sumptuous aria in itself; there could be no better contrast than the Metropolitan Opera's stylized depiction of its own famous facade, one of the best-known performing arts spaces in the world.

The Berkeley Repertory Theatre's configuration of applauding hands creates a universal shorthand for theatrical achievement and approbation, and the Dallas Opera's unique symbol would obviously be out of place anywhere *but* at a musical institution. A graphic signature in the performing arts deserves an equivalent amount of care and attention to that which a company would spend on the design of a set or costume— perhaps even more, since the corporate signature has a life far beyond that of a passing production.

1
The Guthrie Theater
News release masthead
Designer: Nancy Gardner
Agency: Markgraf & Wells
Marketing & Advertising, Inc.

2
The Guthrie Theater
Designer: Rob Ray Kelley

3
Tulsa Opera
Designer: Jim Davies
Agency: Hinkle-Crawford-Davies

4
Metropolitan Opera
Designer: Holley Flagg

5
Berkeley Repertory Theatre
Designer: Jerry Hayworth

6
Chelsea Theater Center
Designer: Dorothy Koda

7
Hippodrome Theatre
Designer: Marshall New

8
Dallas Civic Opera
Design: The Richards Group

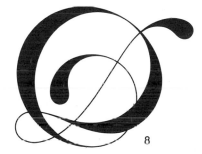

The most frequent and personalized contact an organization makes with the outside world usually appears on its business letterhead. In this area, a performing arts group has the option of being theatrical or functional—complementing performance, or contrasting with it.

Here we see two contrasting examples of letterheads employed by a pair of New England arts groups. The Yale Repertory Theatre's no-nonsense system—including business cards, news release paper and even a newsletter design—represents a functional use of typography embellished only with the accenting of the company's more familiar name—Yale Rep—and some resulting wordplay on the newsletter. The deliberate decision has been made to avoid making any "artistic" statement.

On the other hand, witness the Hartford Symphony's explosive use of image and color. The illustration is a photo-enlargement of the three opening notes of Beethoven's Fifth Symphony, printed in warm tones of brown and orange. Such an audacious approach, of course, usually necessitates extreme restraint in typography. (The company tells us they considered taking the treatment one playful step further—a second sheet for two-page letters containing the *concluding* note of Beethoven's immortal symphonic introduction!)

1

1
Yale Repertory Theatre
Designer: Cynthia Friedman

2
Hartford Symphony Orchestra
Designer: Peter Good

**Hartford
Symphony
Orchestra**

470
Capitol
Avenue

Hartford
Connecticut
06106

Phone:
203
278-1453

Arthur Winograd,
Music Director
and Conductor

Thomas Philion,
Managing Director

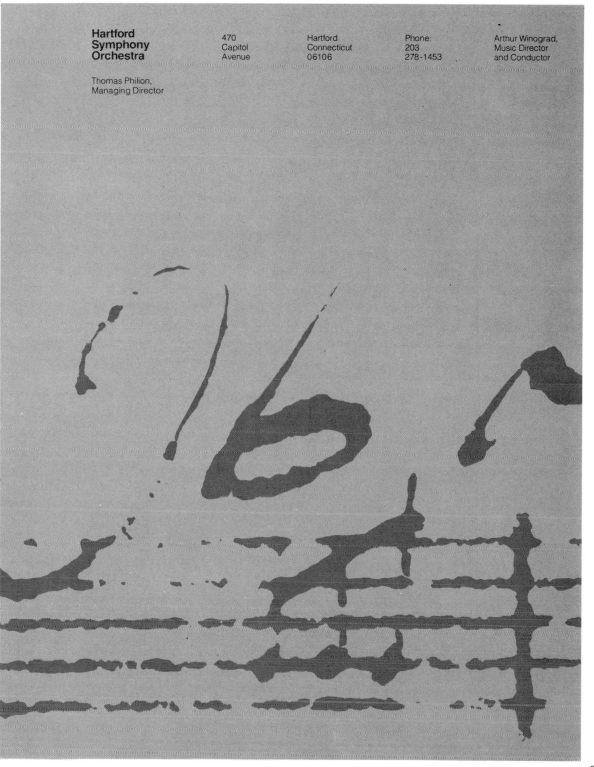

2

Successful letterheads communicate the personality of their organization. Here, the Los Angeles Shakespeare Festival (now known as the Free Public Theatre Festival L.A.) makes a statement that could be made nowhere but in Southern California; New Dramatists communicates its role as a *writer's* theatre instantly; and the Berkeley Repertory Theatre's letterhead combines a clean-edged, contemporary treatment with a classical symmetry—a good description, in its way, of the company's artistic direction and goals.

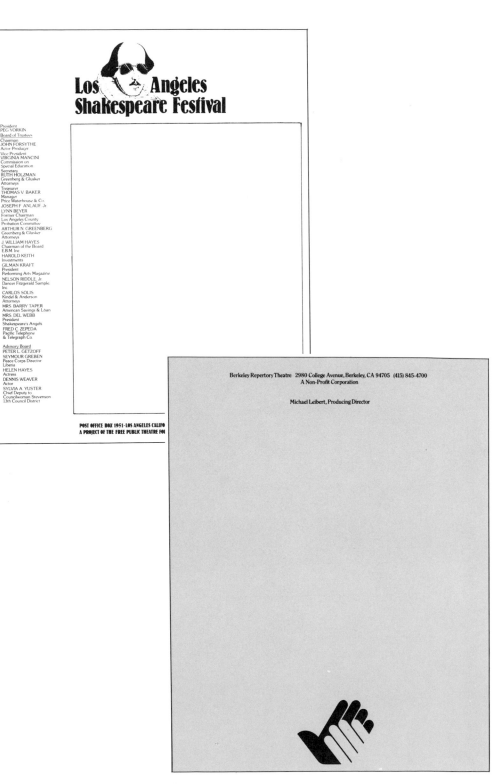

1

1

Los Angeles Shakespeare Festival
Designer: Bonita Rosenblum

2

Berkeley Repertory Theatre
Designer: Jerry Hayworth

3

New Dramatists
Staff Creative Director: John Nassivera
Agency: Ash/LeDonne, Inc.

2

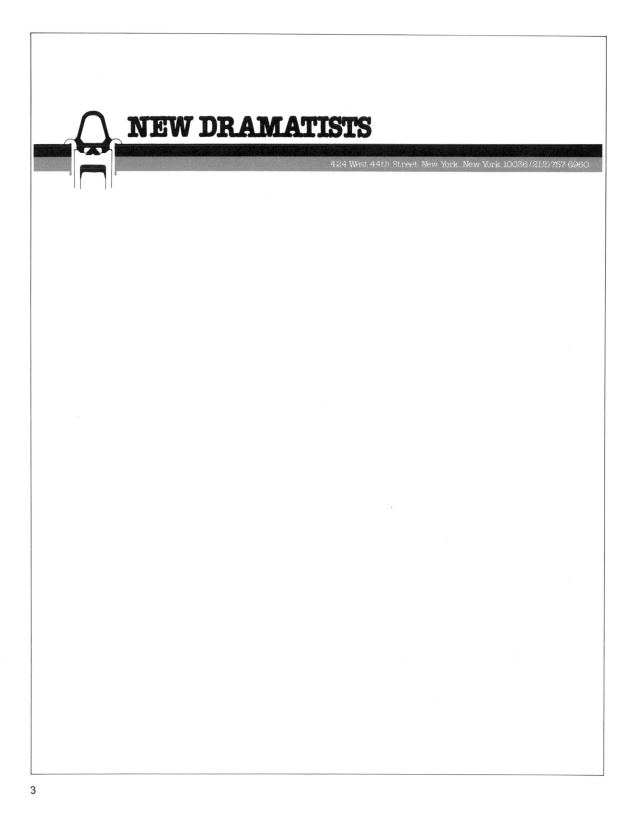

NEW DRAMATISTS

424 West 44th Street, New York, New York 10036 (212) 757-6960

3

One of the performing arts' leading design advocates has been Craig Palmer, former creative director of the New York-based Palmer Communications and now head of marketing for Seattle's Fifth Avenue Theatre. Palmer's modern, clean-lined style has found favor with performing troupes from New England to the Pacific Northwest, and with good reason—his work combines a rare visual integrity with an up-to-the-minute grasp of contemporary marketing trends: Palmer's designs are elegant, visually economical and effective.

"It's a shame that so many performing groups spend a lot of time clarifying their artistic goals on stage, and then discard them in print," says Palmer. "A good art director is the equivalent of an artistic director—except that he extends the language of the performance *beyond* the performance."

Palmer points out that "most people form their impressions of performing arts groups from secondary sources—comments of friends, posters, advertising and the like—not from actual performances. A good design system, therefore, serves to motivate and reinforce these secondary impressions. A strong visibility base is especially important to touring companies which frequently have no *other* visibility than advance promotional materials."

In developing a design concept, Palmer urges organizations to be a little far-sighted. "Presenting yourself as 'a small company on the way up' can be a trap, especially if you intend to grow beyond that role." He often asks his clients how they envision themselves "two or three years down the line." He also tries to interview several people connected with the client organization before making a presentation—staff members, artistic

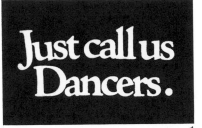

directors, board members, as well as an objective but concerned outside person, such as a foundation executive.

Palmer feels that an identity system should be rethought about every three years. "The first year of a new design is to catch people's attention, the second to make them accustomed to it, and the third to solidify the impression. It's very important that an arts group seem fresh and dynamic in the public eye, and three years is probably about the longest that a particular graphic identity can be useful."

Another reason for periodic changes in graphics is that "arts groups tend to molt; they're always shedding their skins and redefining themselves artistically. Good design systems can herald and support such a change."

Palmer is aware that nonprofit organizations are being forced to compete one-on-one with other leisure activities for a tighter entertainment dollar. "Since a nonprofit group is unlikely to be able to *afford* anything more than printed promotion, quality graphic design becomes centrally important. Broadcast is growing, but print communications will be primary for most cultural groups for a long time."

For all the rewards of working for arts groups, there are frustrations as well. "There is a tendency for people who are creative in one medium to imagine that they are automatically expressive in other media as well," says Palmer. "But choreographing a ballet and designing a brochure are two completely different activities, even though one supports the other. The best artists are comfortable within their own areas of expertise, and give the graphic designer the same amount of latitude and support they extend to other creative professionals.

"I still encounter frustrations, but when I do, I try to handle them creatively."

Pennsylvania Ballet

OHIO BALLET

5

1–5

Design Firm: Palmer Communications
Creative Director: Craig Palmer
Art Directors: Gene Massimo, Tom Dolle
and John Keller

1

Dennis Wayne's Dancers
Teeshirt design

2

Fifth Avenue Theatre
Logo

3

Jacob's Pillow Dance Festival
Logo

4

Pennsylvania Ballet
Logo

5

Ohio Ballet
Logo

4

Craig Palmer

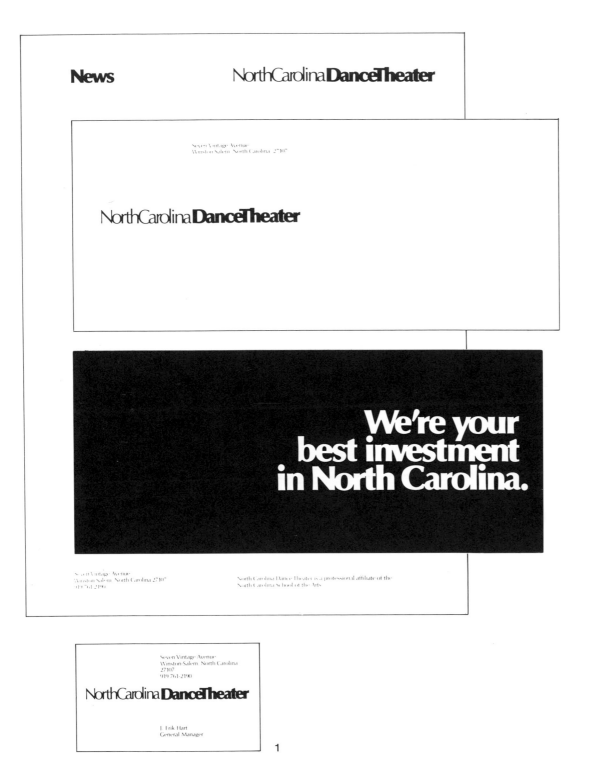

"Attractive...with eclectic repertory... they excelled in works by Balanchine and Tudor." NEW YORK TIMES

North Carolina **Dance Theater is coming.**

Robert Lindgren, Artistic Director

North Carolina Dance Theater is a professional affiliate of the North Carolina School of the Arts.

See the Dance Theater tonight.

North Carolina **Dance Theater tickets now.**

1,2
North Carolina Dance Theatre
Identity system and advertising formats
Design Firm: Palmer Communications

2

In his fourteen-year tenure as producing director of the Hartford (Conn.) Stage Company, Paul Weidner was one of the first artistic directors to emphasize a consistently high level of graphic achievement in his institution's promotional materials and publications—an achievement he closely links to artistic goals.

"I happen to like graphics and design, and maybe that's why I paid a lot of attention to them for the Stage Company. Even so, the graphics of a theatre—which are often the very first thing about that theatre that anybody sees—are without question a substantial part of the artistic image that the company projects. Whether you're sleek and glamorous, or warehousey and burlapish, the kind of audience you want—and even how you want to look to people who have no intention of ever going to the theatre—all can be said right up front just through the use of a typeface.

"I've come to think, too, that you're better off with one person doing it all. Graphic design by committee is about as effective as choosing a season that way. One artist, who knows the particular theatre and is sympathetic to it, should lay out the basic book—needless to say with the approval of the artistic director; that look should be applicable to all the graphic needs of the theatre, and it should be followed through as consistently and doggedly as Coca Cola hangs on to its own dependable trademark."

1

2

3

4

It's A Kick!

The Hartford
Stage Company's
Great New
Season! 527-5151

Ted Graeber, Jeffrey Jones
and Henry Thomas
in A Flea in Her Ear
Photo: Lanny Nagler
Design: William Wondriska

Thanks To United Technologies For Making This Poster Possible

5

1
Rehearsal sketch of Paul Weidner
by Victoria Zussin

2
Hartford Stage Company
Editorial layout, *On the Scene*
magazine
Designer: David J. Skal

3–5
Hartford Stage Company
Subscription materials, 1975-78
Designer: William Wondriska

6
Hartford Stage Company
Corporate logo
Designer: William Wondriska

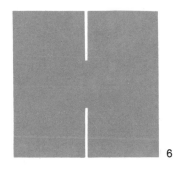

6

Possibly more than any other theatre institution in the country, Joseph Papp's New York Shakespeare Festival has consistently created a level of graphic identification as respected in its own right as the Festival's innovative work onstage. In addition to a strong, durable identity system and trend-setting ad campaigns, the series of Paul Davis posters for such productions as *The Cherry Orchard, For Colored Girls . . ., Streamers* and others became instant classics, prompting the Festival's former associate director Bernard Gersten to comment, "What Toulouse Lautrec did for the Moulin Rouge, Paul Davis is doing for the New York Shakespeare Festival."

1

2

3

5

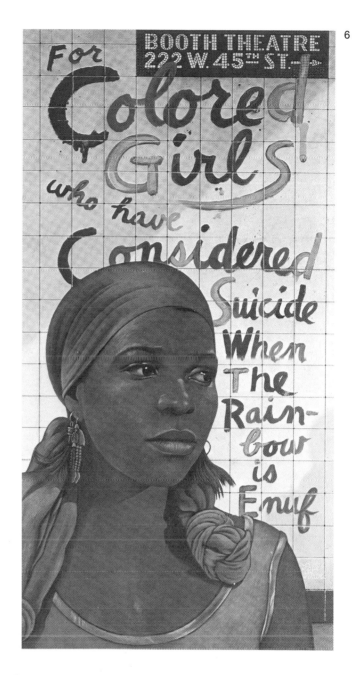

6

1
Festival symbol
Design: Case & McGrath, Inc.

2
Poster
Photo montage: Paul Elson and
Martha Swope
Agency: Serino, Coyne & Nappi, Inc.

3
Festival banner
Designer: Susan Frank

4
Mailing label
Creative Director: Nancy Heller
Agency: Serino, Coyne & Nappi, Inc.

5,6
Posters
Illustrator: Paul Davis
Art Director: Reinhold Schwenk
Agency: Case & McGrath, Inc.

SPOKESONG

SEATTLE REPERTORY THEATRE

MARCH 19 TO APRIL 13 1980

SPOKESONG

OR THE COMMON WHEEL

BY STEWART PARKER

Posters, Illustration and Display Advertising

It's been often noted that a performance on stage is ephemeral, that no two performances of any production are ever quite the same, that the connection between artist and audience happens just once and then survives only in memory.

Anyone who works in the theatre is aware of the profound sense of nostalgia that pervades the industry. The desire to recapture the past—or at least to hold on to its memory—may account for our continued fascination with the theatrical poster. The poster has been many things in its history: an advertising workhorse, a decorative embellishment, political propaganda—and finally, a crumbling souvenir, carefully preserved. Few elements of a production survive the final curtain; sets are struck, companies disband and audiences go home. The poster alone has staying power.

The poster is no longer central to the promotion of the performing arts. Mass communications have rendered most uses of the poster as obsolete as movable type. While Broadway posters dominate subway and train stations from Boston to Washington they are only a form of backup to the massive television advertising that is required to "sell" a Broadway production in the 1980s. Institutional theatres, dance and opera companies all know that their best hopes for attracting audiences lie with direct-mail brochures and scrupulously maintained computer printouts of the names, addresses, and income levels of potential patrons.

But the poster persists. Richard Frankel, who heads public relations for New York's influential Circle Repertory Company, puts it this way: "We don't print posters in order to sell tickets—we print them for the same reason we build sets and design costumes. It's part of the total artistic product. It's part of what we do." The notion of the poster as an artistic discipline in itself is a distinctly European one, as we will see.

The modern poster was essentially a product of the industrial revolution, resulting from advances in nineteenth century lithography and the ability of automated printing presses to print posters in large quantities. During the *Belle Epoque*, posters became a major form of urban decoration in Europe, were made the subject of books and exhibitions, and were highly sought after by collectors.

The poster has been central not only to the performing arts, but to political movements and revolutions as well. Because it is such a visual art form, it has been highly useful in marshalling large social movements across linguistic and geographical boundaries—witness the powerful use of poster iconography in modern China.

American design professionals have long decried the "visual neglect" rampant in our society, and similar complaints are standard in virtually every other creative discipline. In the performing arts especially this previous lack of graphic legitimacy can be linked to a deep-seated distrust of the theatre itself.

In his excellent survey, *The Art of the Broadway Poster* (Ballantine), Michael Patrick Hearn tells us, "The early American theatre encouraged the anonymity of its artists. Nineteenth-century Puritans disapproved of the stage; many Americans agreed with Horace Greeley that the theatres were 'moral pest houses'... many performers were forced to adopt stage names to protect their families' reputations. Similarly, those who designed theatre posters generally

1

Seattle Repertory Theatre
Designer/illustrator: William Cumming

did not sign their work." Hearn also reports that an 1899 edition of the magazine *The Poster* complained "that most of the theatrical posters are hideous ... goes without saying," and that poster design had fallen to the level of patent medicine advertising.

Theatre posters in the United States have never attained the artistic prominence that they have in Europe. Though Broadway poster designers have long claimed an affectionate "camp" following, relatively few posters have really transcended their commercial intentions. (The remarkable, eccentric Theatre Guild posters of the 1930s and '40s are a notable exception.) The 1960s gave American graphic arts a major shot in the arm, and since that time we

have seen some of the theatre's most innovative poster designs, including the work of Paul Davis, Gilbert Lesser, David Byrd, Edward Gorey and others.

While the golden age of poster advertising is over, posters and poster-like approaches to promotional materials are still with us. In revitalized urban centers all over the United States, there is a revival of interest in urban decoration— banners and posters proliferate, perhaps as an antidote to "mass" culture. Newspaper advertisements are miniature posters themselves, and poster techniques are to be found in abundance on direct-mail brochures, in display advertising, and on the covers of playbills.

In the media-saturated "global

village," our town squares and poster walls have been largely supplanted by television cables, data banks and satellite-transmitted newspaper layouts. Obviously, an effective poster design in the 1980s should be able to withstand translation into other media—newspaper ads, mass transit cards, even television animation. (Both newspaper and television are "low resolution" media, and perhaps this explains the rise of the simplified, high-contrast logotype that can withstand the poorest reproduction or broadcast distortion.)

The poster has proved to be a stubbornly durable spokesman for the performing arts. Over 100 years after its birth, it is still speaking as loudly as ever, as the following chapter demonstrates.

1

3

1
Cleveland Playhouse
Posters, circa 1920

2
Seattle Repertory Theatre
Designer: Ellen Ziegler, with
Mark Michaelson
Photographer: Jim Cummins

3
The 1940's Radio Hour
Designer: Paul de Pass
Client: Jujamcyn Theaters Corporation

1

2

3

The difference between highly polished commercial graphics and the results achievable in the nonprofit institution is not so great as it may seem. In fact, if the work of airbrush illustrator Doug Johnson is any indication, the gap does not exist at all. One of Johnson's most celebrated designs, the poster for the Broadway revival of *Candide*, was originally created for the Chelsea Theater Center's Brooklyn staging

highly specific." In contrast, many nonprofit organizations are willing to extend considerable creative leeway to an outstanding designer who is willing to work for less than the prevailing industry rates.

Johnson's work for the Chelsea Theater Center was intended "to be a reaction to what everybody else was doing. We tried to make it look as if we were having fun. We were an 'un-theatre' kind of theatre."

The license plate poster design was intended to reinforce the "regionalism" of the theatre's former Brooklyn location; the life preserver symbolized the company's mission to lend new vigor to theatrical art. In addition to the striking illustrations, Johnson also wrote the copy for the Chelsea's subscription materials.

Needless to say, each is a collector's item today—if one can be found.

1

of the play. When the show moved to Broadway, the poster followed as a fixture of the production.

Johnson, a highly successful illustrator whose assignments regularly include record album covers, magazine covers, movie posters and the like, maintains an interest in the decidedly nonlucrative nonprofit arena largely because of the creative latitude afforded him there. "In most advertising situations, the illustrator has no latitude whatsoever," he says. "The demands are

2

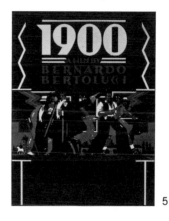

1–5
Art Director/Illustrator: Doug Johnson
Design Firm: Performing Dogs

1, 3, 4
Chelsea Theater Center

2
Ain't Misbehavin'
Agency: Serino, Coyne and Nappi, Inc.

5
1900
Client: Paramount Pictures

In Eastern Europe, where the theatre provides a public forum as well as entertainment, the poster occupies a special cultural and artistic position. According to Daniel C. Gerould, who co-directed a major 1980 exhibition of Polish and Soviet theatre posters at the Graduate Center of the City University of New York: "In Eastern European countries, theatre posters do not simply serve to announce current and coming attractions; they are an art form in themselves. The theatre poster is designed as urban decoration and beautification, as visual education, and as comment on and complement to the creative work taking place on stage.

"In Poland, the theatre poster is a means of artistic expression rather than a commercial enterprise to promote business. Each Polish theatre attempts to establish a distinctive style for its posters

and to have its artists follow certain common principles of format, lettering or use of an identifying symbol, no matter how diverse their individual talents. The aim is to produce a kind of poster immediately recognizable as belonging to a given theatre."

The Polish poster artist, says Gerould, is usually active in other branches of the graphic arts, and scenic designers will frequently create posters themselves.

In the Soviet Union, according to exhibit co-director Alma H. Law, theatrical posters have provided graphic designers with a means of reaching beyond the limits of Socialist Realist art in order to embrace some of the major contemporary trends in Western art. "Today, Soviet theatrical posters are characterized by an enormous range of idioms, from the surreal to the sentimental. Whatever their artistic style, how-

ever, the best of them share a strong desire to convey the essence of the theatrical production.

"As a number of critics have pointed out, the use of metaphor and associative imagery has become one of the major means of representing the theme of a production. The use of allegory in poster art is nothing new, of course, but as audiences have become better educated and more sophisticated, the potential for its use has grown enormously. This explains in part why many theatrical posters convey a more accurate and vivid picture of a production's meaning than do photographs of it."

Western specialists have long recognized the special vibrancy and excitement of the graphic arts in the Soviet bloc countries; the performing arts in particular have few better sources of visual innovation and energy.

1

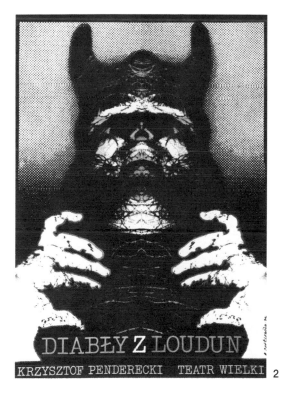

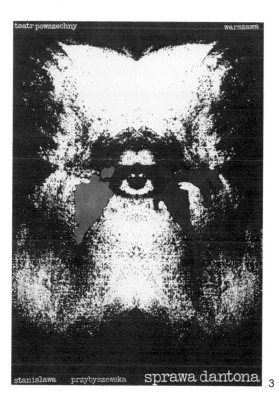

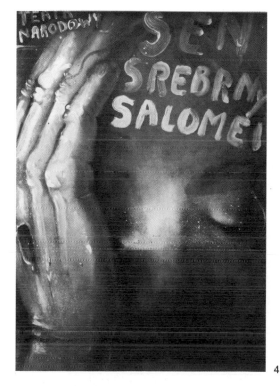

1
Poster for International Theatre Day, 1977
Designer: Jerzy Czerniawski

2
Teatr Wielki, Warsaw
Poster for *The Devils of Loudon*
Designer: Roman Cieślewicz

3
Teatr Powszechny, Warsaw
Poster for *The Danton Case*
Designer: Roman Cieślewicz

4
The National Theatre, Warsaw
Poster for *The Silver Dream of Salomea*
Designer: Jerzy Czerniawski

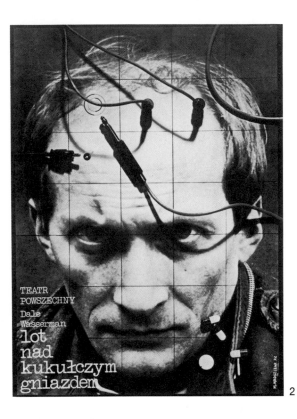

5

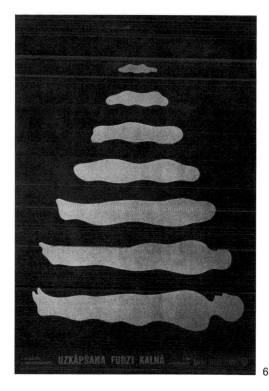

6

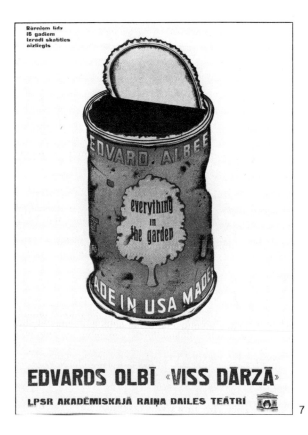

7

1
Teatre Powszechny, Warsaw
Poster for *The House of Bernarda Alba*
Designer: Janusz Wiśniewski

2
Teatr Powszechny, Warsaw
Poster for *One Flew Over the Cuckoo's Nest*
Designer: Marcin Mroszczak

3
Lenin Komsomol Theatre, Leningrad
Poster for *The Lark*
Designer: Victor K. Kundyshev

4
Maly Opera and Ballet Theatre, Leningrad
Poster for *Yaroslavna*
Designer: S. Zakharyants

5
Central Children's Theatre, Moscow
Poster for *Twelfth Night*
Designer: Edward P. Zmoiro

6
Yan Rainis Art Theatre, Riga
Poster for *The Ascent of Mount Fuji*
Designer: Ilmars Blumberg

7
Yan Rainis Art Theatre, Riga
Poster for *Everything in the Garden*
Designer: Ilmars Blumberg

Under the direction of resident theatre pioneer Zelda Fichandler, the Arena Stage in Washington, D.C. has long shown an interest in new plays from Eastern Europe and, not surprisingly, has also adopted a distinctly European approach to theatre posters. Throughout the early 1970's, poster artist John Barber created original, limited-edition silkscreen posters for each major production, based on sketches and impressions gathered at dress rehearsals and completed for opening nights. The posters were sold to patrons in the theatre lobby before and after performances and the artist kept all proceeds in lieu of a fee. Arena Stage, meanwhile, benefited from the "soft" public relations effect of having its name and productions framed and hung in people's homes, as well as from a stunning lobby display reflecting years of theatrical achievement at a glance.

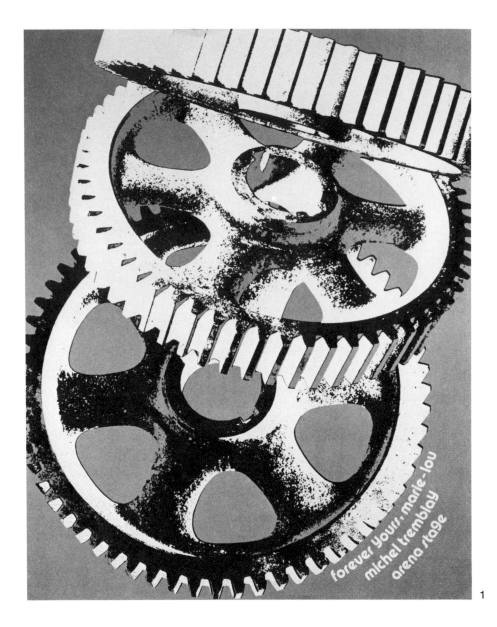

1

1-6

Arena Stage
Designer: John Barber

LONG DAY'S JOURNEY INTO NIGHT

ARENA STAGE — O'NEILL

2

3

THORNTON WILDER   ARENA STAGE

OUR TOWN

4

THE FRONT PAGE

B. HECHT
C. MAC ARTHUR
ARENA STAGE

5

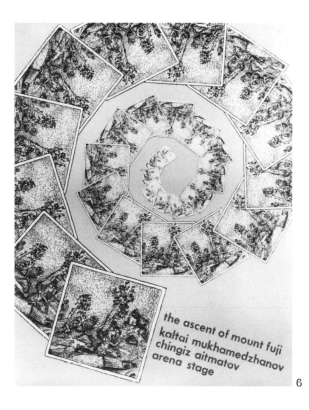

the ascent of mount fuji
kaltai mukhamedzhanov
chingiz aitmatov
arena stage

6

1

Cincinnati Ballet
Designer: Dan Bittman
Photographer: Jack Kauck
Agency: Sive Associates, Inc.

2

San Francisco Ballet
Designer/Sculptor: Norman Orr
Design Firm: Jaciow, Kelley and Orr, Inc.

1

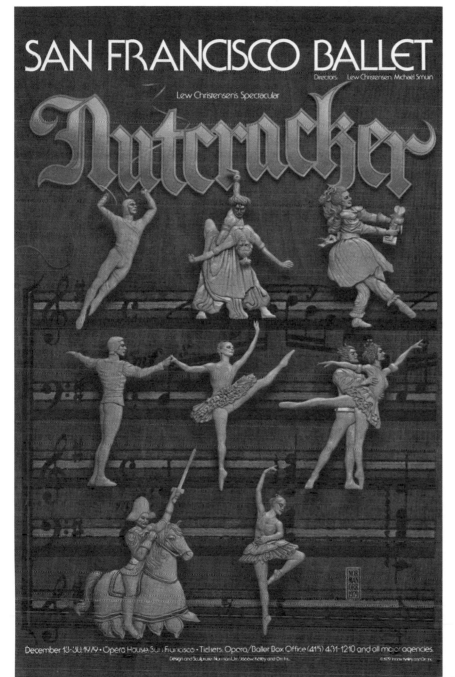

2

Adaptations of Charles Dickens' *A Christmas Carol* have become to resident theatre companies what *The Nutcracker* is to the ballet world—a festive source of holiday bounty. And graphic designers have been enjoying the merriment as much as anyone.

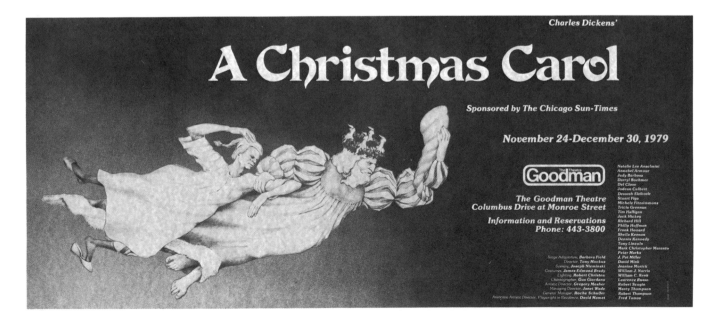

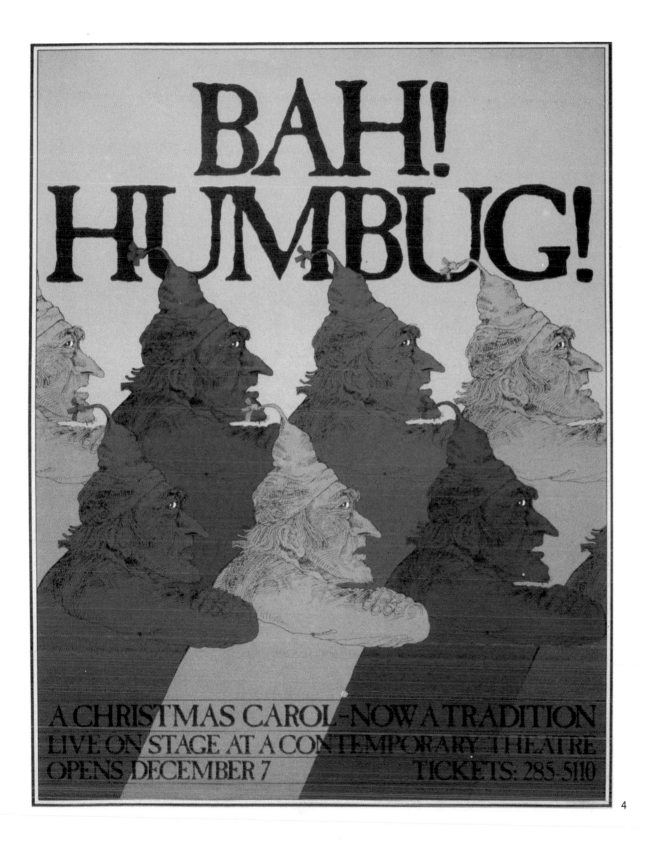

BAH! HUMBUG!

A CHRISTMAS CAROL-NOW A TRADITION
LIVE ON STAGE AT A CONTEMPORARY THEATRE
OPENS DECEMBER 7   TICKETS: 285-5110

4

Theatre Three
Designer: Dean Corbitt

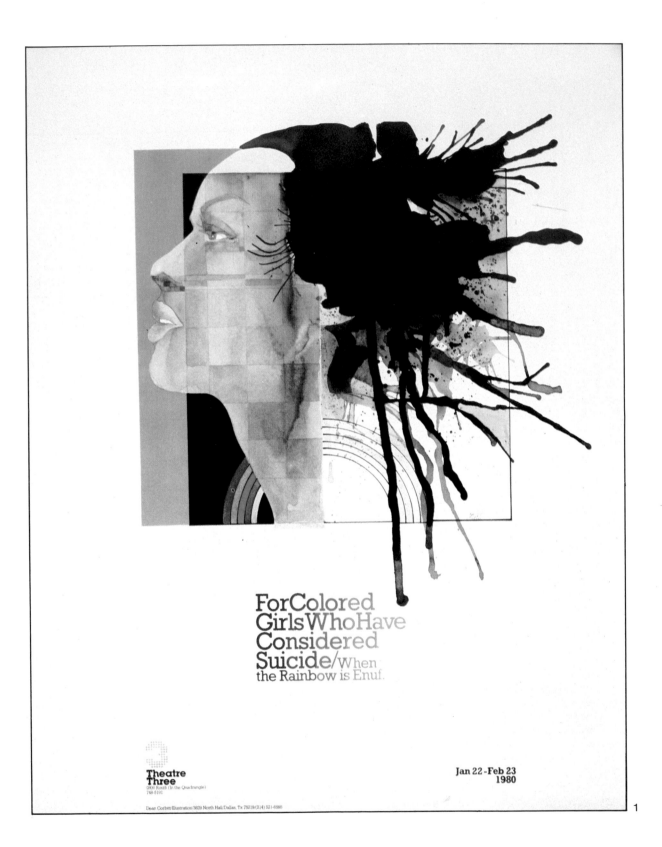

ForColored
GirlsWhoHave
Considered
Suicide/When
the Rainbow is Enuf.

**Theatre
Three**
2800 Routh (In the Quadrangle)
748-5191

Jan 22 - Feb 23
1980

Dean Corbitt/Illustration/3629 North Hall/Dallas, Tx 75219/(214) 521-6986

1

2

Indianapolis Symphony
Designer: Richard Listenberger
Photographer: Joseph McGuire

3

Mark Taper Forum
Design: John Miyauchi and Associates

4

Oregon Shakespearean Festival
Photographer: Hank Kranzler

5

INTAR
Designer: Randy Barcelo

2

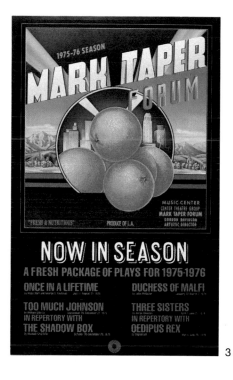

3

4

5

1
_____
Million Dollar Theatre
Handbill

2
_____
Mark Taper Forum
Design: John Follis and Associates
Illustrator: Ignacio Gomez

Kenneth Brecher, whose anthropological fieldwork in the Amazon formed the basis and guided the London and Los Angeles productions of Christopher Hampton's play *Savages*, was invited by Gordon Davidson to become associate artistic director at the Mark Taper Forum, where his concern with cultural diversity continued to influence his work. In collaboration with graphic designers, he helped evolve a striking new approach to theatre graphics intended to reach a special audience reflecting the ethnic mix of a complex metropolitan community.

Zoot Suit, Luis Valdez's play about ethnic identity and racial conflict in the Los Angeles of the 1940s, was the first play to address the concerns of the Hispanic population of that city that reached a large audience. After a smashingly successful run at the Taper, the play was moved to a larger theatre, the Aquarius, where it broke house records week after week for more than four months. The show attracted unprecedented attendance by segments of the Hispanic community that had rarely, if ever, been among the traditional Los Angeles theatre audience in the past.

The play's success was underpinned by a brilliant media campaign—in which the principles of anthropology supported an effective cross-cultural communication effort. Brecher brought the skills of an anthropologist to the task of identifying and assessing the community he wanted to reach.

A key principle was Brecher's realization that traditional theatre graphics originate in a very specialized segment of society. "I thought: people who are recognized as leaders in graphics are doing these things, but they're not coming from the communities that I would like to attract to this theatre." The Taper therefore found and employed artists from within the communities that *were* Brecher's targets. "These artists brought with them a sensibility which one could never have artificially imposed on those posters. One of the things I learned, specifically from a trip down to the Million Dollar Theatre in Los Angeles, where the big Spanish acts play, was that people got flyers announcing coming attractions. They had

1

wonderful rippled colors—it's called the 'split fountain' effect." Brecher connected this discovery with the Taper's production of *Zoot Suit* in order to make information about the production more accessible to the community whose artifact he was borrowing. "What if, behind the figure of El Pachuco in *Zoot Suit*, in the background was the Los Angeles skyline, but *in the split fountain effect?* What if we used that turquoise which is maybe not design-conference turquoise but *is* pure East L.A.? Would it read as *real*,

not just white liberals doing their thing to bring in Hispanic audiences?" It did, and illustrator Ignacio Gomez's painting became an instant classic. "A sense of the idea's effectiveness comes from the fact that people save those posters and use them and recognize them," says Brecher.

Once designed, the posters must be distributed. "Where you put them is important," says Brecher. "Some theatres might think it beneath them to put up posters on telephone poles. What does it *mean*, when you're doing professional work and winning awards, to have somebody in a shopping mall handing out flyers like a *little* theatre? What do these flyers mean? And what do they say? To attract a certain audience they would say 'Pulitzer Prize-winning Author'; for another, 'Exciting New World Premiere'; for still another, 'The Noel Coward We Love.'

"But what if the flyer said, 'Twenty-three Actors for $4.50'? We need to let people know what they're getting for their money, though perhaps in a less vulgar way. Answer questions. *Who's* on that stage? Are they going to like those people? Can they identify with them? People don't ask themselves those questions consciously; it's a gut feeling.

"I don't feel I'm saying anything that people don't already know. It's like all those truths that one finds in the work of anthropologists—the most profound things are the ones that are the most obvious once they've been stated. But when people know what they're getting for their money it makes a tremendous difference; and graphics become very important in letting them know."

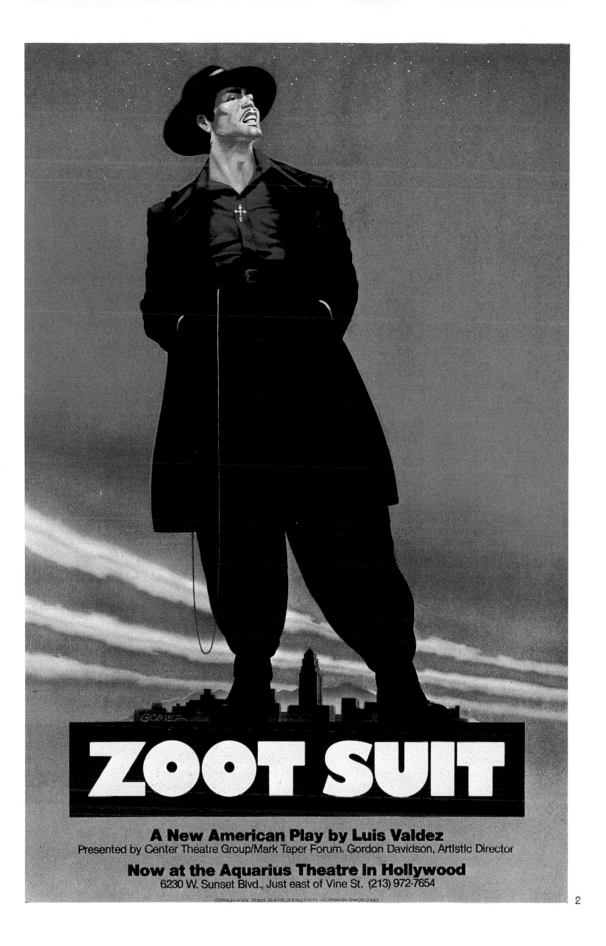

ZOOT SUIT

A New American Play by Luis Valdez
Presented by Center Theatre Group/Mark Taper Forum. Gordon Davidson, Artistic Director

Now at the Aquarius Theatre in Hollywood
6230 W. Sunset Blvd., Just east of Vine St. (213) 972-7654

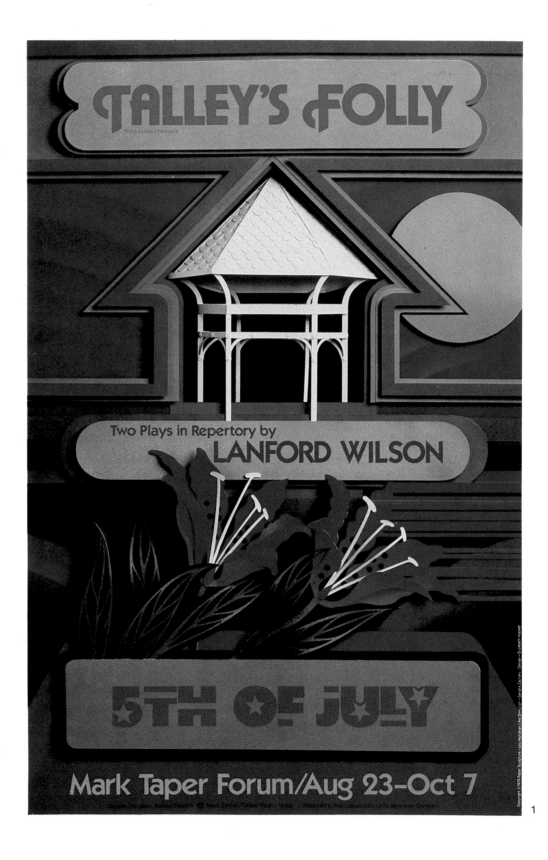

1
Mark Taper Forum
Designer: Elizabeth Kooker
Paper Sculpture: Leo Monahan
Creative Director: Sandra Zachary
Agency: Ogilvy and Mather

2
Hartford Stage Company
Illustration for *A History of the American Film*
Construction: David J. Skal
Photographer: Lanny Nagler

3
Repertory Dance Theatre
Postcard
Designer: Marina Harris

2

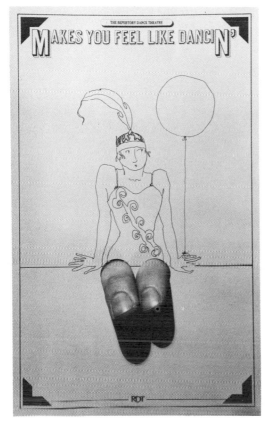

3

Some of the most colorful and exuberant images for the performing arts come with delirious frequency from The Children's Theatre Company and School in Minneapolis. Steven Rydberg's fanciful illustrations are the basis for posters, postcards and publication covers. They effectively—and charmingly—extend the troupe's unique identity beyond the stage and into the community.

1–5
Children's Theatre Company and School
Posters and Illustrations
Designer/Illustrator: Steven Rydberg

2

1

3

4

5

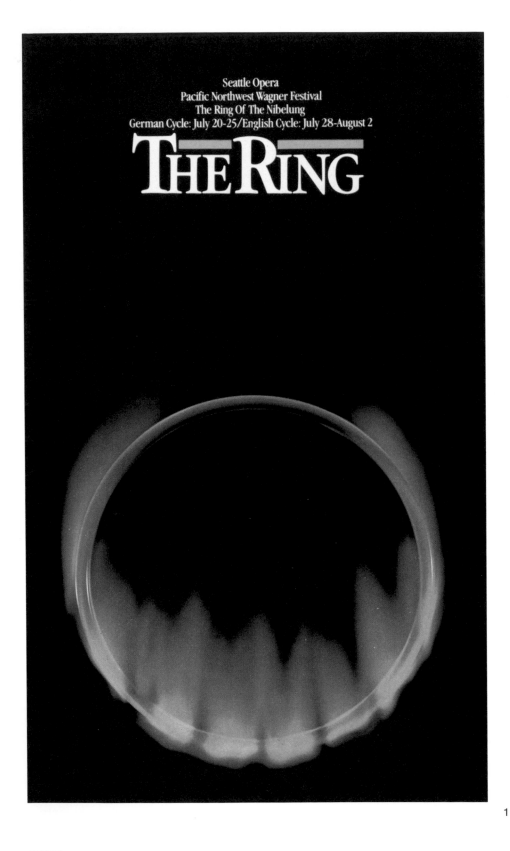

Seattle Opera
Pacific Northwest Wagner Festival
The Ring Of The Nibelung
German Cycle: July 20-25/English Cycle: July 28-August 2

THE RING

1

Seattle Opera
Designer: Gregory J. Erickson
Illustrator: Al Doggett
Photographer: Walter Hodges
Creative Director: Cynthia C. Hartwig
Agency: Sharp, Hartwig & Vladimir
(Seattle)

2

Lyric Opera of Chicago
Commemorative Tapestries
Designer: Norman Laliberté

3

Metropolitan Opera
Designer: David Byrd
Agency: Walter Pfaf, Inc.

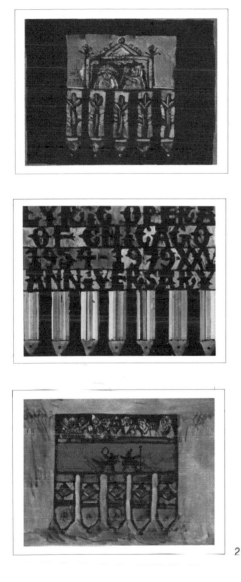

2

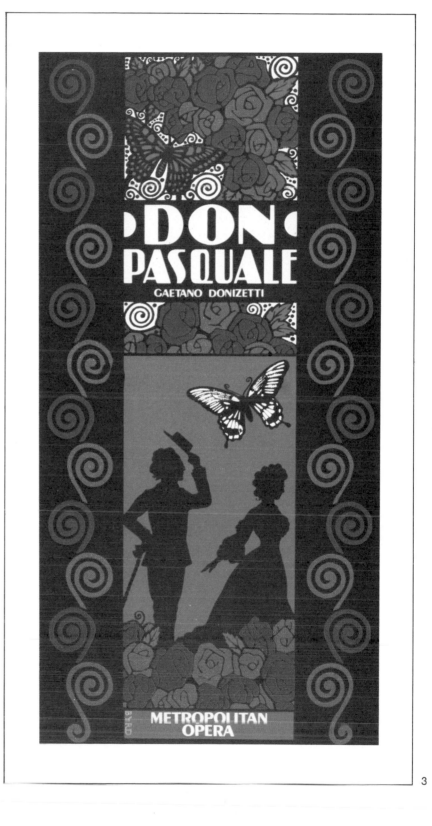

3

Called "The New Medicis" by the *Saturday Review*, American corporations are becoming a significant source of funding for the arts. It is not surprising, therefore, that an increasing number of outstanding designs for the performing arts are the result of direct corporate sponsorship.

The partnership is a natural one—public relations people at nonprofit arts organizations have little money for "prestige" posters and designs, while the public relations people of large corporations do have the money, and are often delighted to associate their corporate identities with the creative arts.

Based in Hartford, Connecticut, United Technologies Corporation has been a leader in corporate sponsorship of fine graphics for a variety of cultural groups. According to Gordon Bowman, director of Corporate Creative Programs for the $10 billion conglomerate, "some corporations sponsor outboard motor races. United Technologies has chosen the arts as the vehicle for spreading its name. We want the public to associate United Technologies with quality and imagination, and the arts are a perfect means."

Bowman came to United Technologies in the fall of 1977 from Mobil Oil, where he had been the creative director behind Mobil's promotion of its public television series *Masterpiece Theatre*. His first assignment was to improve the overall quality of United Technolgies' corporate graphics and visibility, a responsibility that soon included the sponsorship of projects for Connecticut's Hartford-based arts institutions. Bowman startled the Hartford arts community by literally ringing doorbells of arts administrators, to ask what United Technologies could do for their organizations. For every project, exhibit or festival it sponsored, United Technologies also earmarked a considerable amount of money for graphic promotion.

The corporation does retain complete creative control over any printed materials it sponsors, but since the artists hired to create posters often include design superstars like Arnold Saks and Ivan Chermayeff, there has been little resistance to the stipulation. In the last few years, United Technologies has moved beyond its Connecticut home base in support of the arts; presently its plans include international touring of art exhibitions and fine arts book publishing.

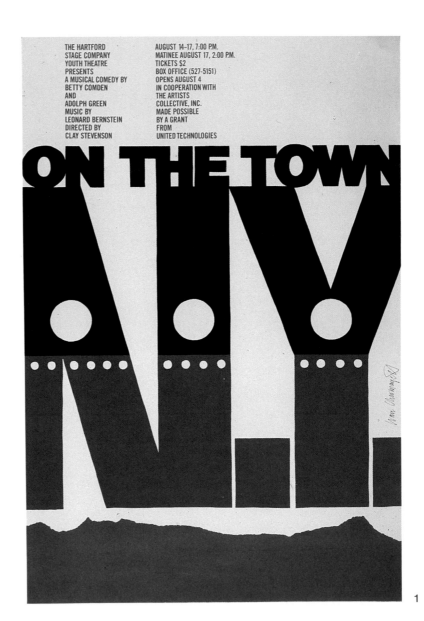

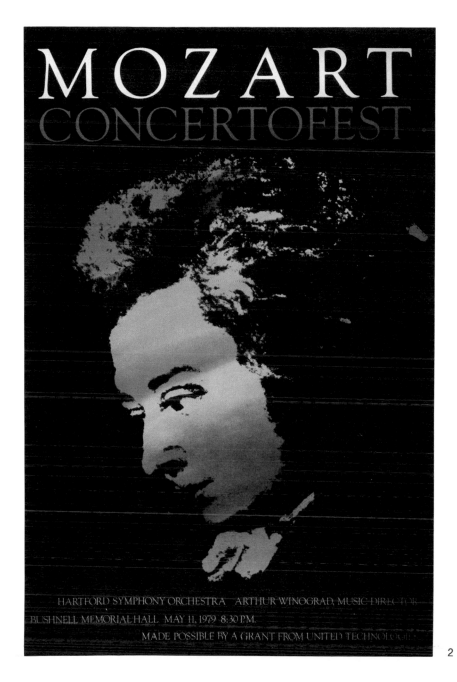

United Technologies Corporation

1
Hartford Stage Company Youth Theatre
Designer: Ivan Chermayeff
Design Firm: Chermayeff and Geismar
Associates
Creative Director: Gordon Bowman

2
Hartford Symphony Orchestra
Designer: Peter Good
Design Firm: Peter Good
Graphic Design
Creative Director: Gordon Bowman

3
Hartford Symphony Orchestra
Designer: William Wondriska
Design Firm: William Wondriska
Associates, Inc.
Creative Director: Gordon Bowman

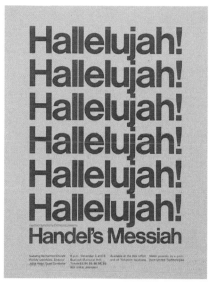

2

3

United Technologies is not the only corporation that has opened new graphic vistas for cultural groups. In Tulsa, Oklahoma, the Phillips Petroleum Company subsidized a handsomely coordinated series of promotional graphics for the Tulsa Opera; two are pictured here. Actor's Theatre of Louisville, home to one of the country's most celebrated new play festivals, attracted the sponsorship of Humana, Inc., a leading hospital supply corporation, which also underwrote a classic photographic evocation of the process of creative writing, reproduced below.

1,3
Tulsa Opera
Designer: Harold Tackett
Illustrator: Jim Davies
Agency: Hinkle-Crawford-Davies
Sponsor: Phillips Petroleum Company

2
Actors Theatre of Louisville
Art Directors: Nathan Felde and
Julius Friedman
Design Firm: Implement, Ltd.
Sponsor: Humana, Inc.

3

2

3

For the Benefit of the
LONDON HOSPITAL.

Royalty Theatre

Well-Street, near Goodman's-Fields.

The PUBLIC are most respectfully informed, that,
On THIS DAY, being JUNE 20, 1787,
The ROYALTY-THEATRE will be OPENED with an

OCCASIONAL ADDRESS,

TO BE DELIVERED BY

Mr. PALMER.

After the ADDRESS will be performed

A COMEDY, called

AS YOU LIKE IT.

To which will be added,

MISS in her TEENS.

BOXES, 5s. PIT, 3s. FIRST GALLERY, 2s. SECOND GALLERY, 1s.

PLACES for the BOXES to be taken at the STAGE-DOOR of the THEATRE,
The DOORS of which will be opened at Half an Hour after FIVE, and the
Performance begin precisely at Half an Hour after SIX o'Clock.

No Money to be returned after the Curtain is drawn up, nor will any Person be
admitted behind the Scenes.   VIVANT REX & REGINA.

N. B. The Frequenters of the Royalty-Theatre, from the West End of the
Town, are hereby informed that there is an excellent Access for Carriages,
from White-Chapel, through Red-Lion Street.

4

1
Illustrator: Dan Long
Agency: Stone Associates, Inc.
Client: *The Shakespeare Plays,* Public
Broadcasting Service

2
Denver Center Theatre Company
Illustrator: Karmen Effenberger-
Thompson

3
Art Direction: Stone Associates, Inc.
Client: *The Shakespeare Plays,* Public
Broadcasting Service

4
Royalty Theatre
Playbill, circa 1787

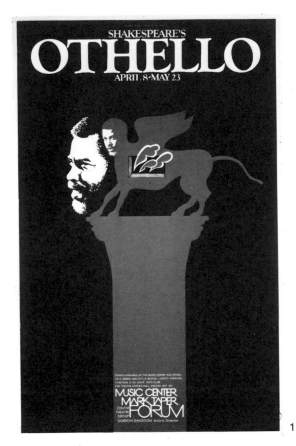

WILLIAM SHAKESPEARE'S
THE TEMPEST

Mark Taper Forum • May 17-July 1
Gordon Davidson, Artistic Director

Fourth Production of the 1978-1979 Season • Music Center Ⓞ Center Theatre Group

4

1
Mark Taper Forum
Designers: Hal Frazier and Paul Thor Hauge
Design Firm: Neumarket Design Associates

2
Brooklyn Academy of Music
Illustrator: Joy Waller

3
Champlain Shakespeare Festival
Illustrator: Michael Patterson

4
Mark Taper Forum
Illustrator: Ignacio Gomez
Art Director: Elizabeth Kooker

1

The Lady from Dubuque
Illustrator: Gary Kendall
Art Director: Don Gordon
Agency: Ash/LeDonne, Inc.

2

University of Nebraska
Designer: Judith Martins

3–4
Texas Opera Theater
Photographer: John Katz
Art Director: David Jenkins
Agency: Ogilvy and Mather

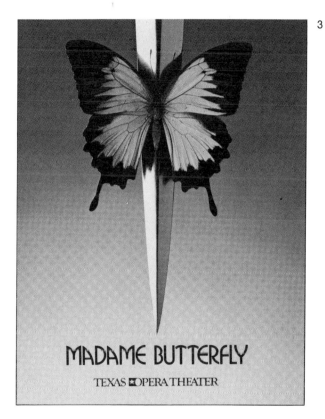

3

MADAME BUTTERFLY

TEXAS OPERA THEATER

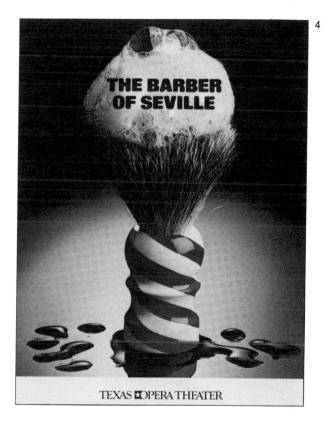

4

THE BARBER OF SEVILLE

TEXAS OPERA THEATER

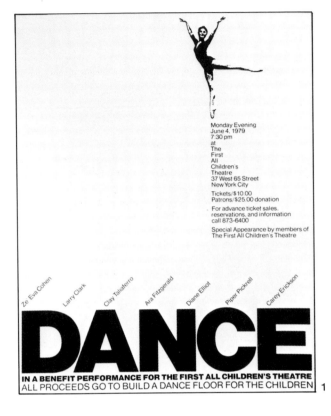

Monday Evening
June 4, 1979
7:30 pm
at
The
First
All
Children's
Theatre
37 West 65 Street
New York City

Tickets/$10.00
Patrons/$25.00 donation

For advance ticket sales,
reservations, and information
call 873-6400

Special Appearance by members of
The First All Children's Theatre

Ze'Eva Cohen Larry Clark Clay Taliaferro Ara Fitzgerald Diane Elliot Piper Pickrell Carey Erickson

DANCE

IN A BENEFIT PERFORMANCE FOR THE FIRST ALL CHILDREN'S THEATRE
ALL PROCEEDS GO TO BUILD A DANCE FLOOR FOR THE CHILDREN 1

1
First All Children's Theatre
Designer: Bruce Duhan

2
New York City Ballet
Designer: Donn Matus

3
Wisconsin Union Theatre
Designer: Susan Grant

2

NIKOLAIS
DANCE THEATRE

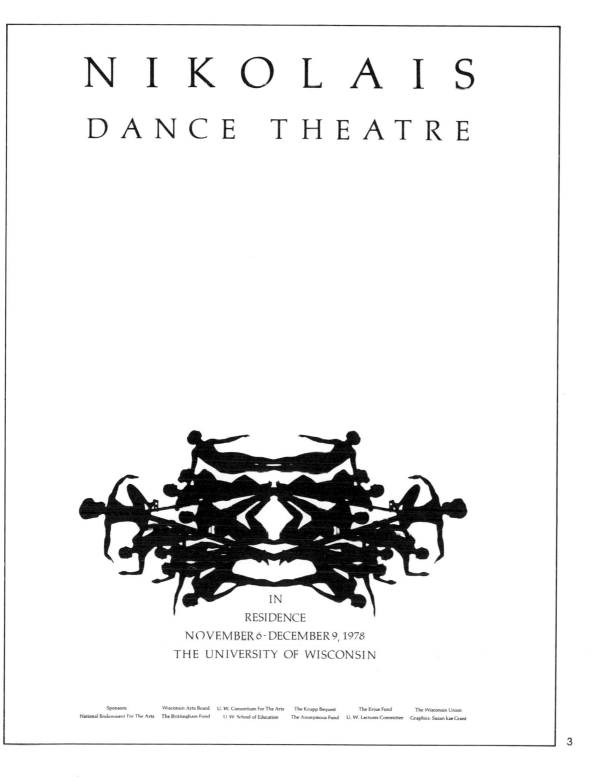

IN
RESIDENCE
NOVEMBER 6 - DECEMBER 9, 1978
THE UNIVERSITY OF WISCONSIN

Sponsors: Wisconsin Arts Board   U. W. Consortium For The Arts   The Knapp Bequest   The Evjue Fund   The Wisconsin Union
National Endowment For The Arts   The Brittingham Fund   U. W. School of Education   The Anonymous Fund   U. W. Lectures Committee   Graphics: Susan kae Grant

3

2

Lewitzky

3

4

Illustration: A Complement to Performance

During its inaugural season, the Denver Center Theatre Company effectively utilized Karmen Effenberger-Thompson's line-drawings in its publications and promotional materials. Thompson executed a coordinated series of illustrations for each of the Center's productions—a stylish complement to performance. The theatre's use of the visuals was equally well-coordinated; Denver theatregoers were treated to the Thompson sketches not only in the company's magazine, advertising, and direct mail brochures, but in the theatre lobby as well, where the original artwork was framed and displayed.

1

Denver Center Theatre Company
Illustrator: Karmen Effenberger-
Thompson

1

The Learned Ladies

2

Moby Dick: A Rehearsal

1

Denver Center Theatre Company
Illustrator: Karmen Effenberger-
Thompson

1
_____
The Caucasian Chalk Circle

2
_____
A Midsummer Night's Dream

2

Often, one outstanding graphic design will inspire others in a similar vein; this is especially likely in the performing arts, where diverse companies produce the same plays but are eager to impart their own visual "stamp" on posters, etc. just as they make individual decisions on casting, set design, and other matters. A classic poster design, such as Paul Davis' work for *Streamers*, is a hard act to follow, but often such an assignment is just the challenge that a good designer is waiting for.

1

2

1

New York Shakespeare Festival
Designer: Paul Davis
Agency: Case & McGrath, Inc.

2

Hippodrome Theatre
Photographer: Jerry N. Uelsmann

3

New York Shakespeare Festival
Art Director: Reinhold Schwenk
Photographer: Jean-Marie Guyaux
Agency: Case & McGrath, Inc.

4

Goodman Theatre
Designer: Joan Stepan
Illustrator: John Sandford

3

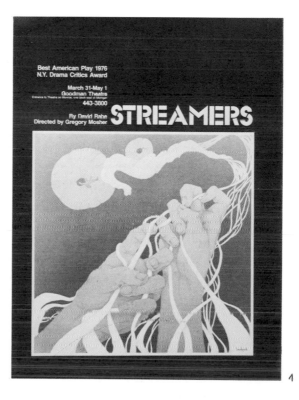

4

Director of Promotion for *Life* magazine and a twenty-year veteran of the Time-Life management team, Gilbert Lesser is also one of America's best known theatre poster designers, thanks to the stark, nearly archetypal images he has created for such productions as *Equus, The Elephant Man, Poor Murderer, Faith Healer* and, most recently, the Broadway reincarnation of the Loretto-Hilton Repertory Theatre's *Frankenstein.* While the ill-fated production closed on opening night, the poster was almost simultaneously selected for inclusion in the Museum of Modern Art's permanent collection.

"I've always done freelance

Gilbert Lesser

work," Lesser says. "And when you do a theatre poster there's that extra little excitement of walking down the street and seing your work up on a wall in public. It's the one time I get to share my work with a broader segment of the population." *Equus* was Lesser's first attempt at a theatre poster, and, while it has since probably come to be as famous as the play itself, it evolved separately and after several false starts. The original London design was discarded before the American premiere, and after a few frustrating attempts with other designers, playwright Peter Shaffer recommended his friend Lesser for the project. He tried several approaches, including a typographical

logo and an intricate "stained-glass" treatment of a horse, both of which gave way to the hard-edged geometry of the final design. The horse's head was originally to be printed in orange and acid green, but Lesser opted for black and white when he learned that one of the play's producers was affected by orange-green color blindness. He prefers black and white in any event.

The Elephant Man, another of Lesser's most memorable designs, represents an attempt to evoke the lead character's distorted physicality without being grotesque. This time, Lesser's instincts were direct. "The

final poster represents the one and only version," he says. "I used the stick figure and torn paper to create a childlike and slightly primitive feeling."

Lesser develops his images through a reading of the script. "Rarely do I talk to anyone involved in the play. The producers of Arthur Miller's *The American Clock* told me that Miller wanted to discuss concepts for the poster, so I made sure to finish it before we even met. When I showed him what I had done, he said 'Well, there's not much use in talking, is there?' But he liked the poster very much."

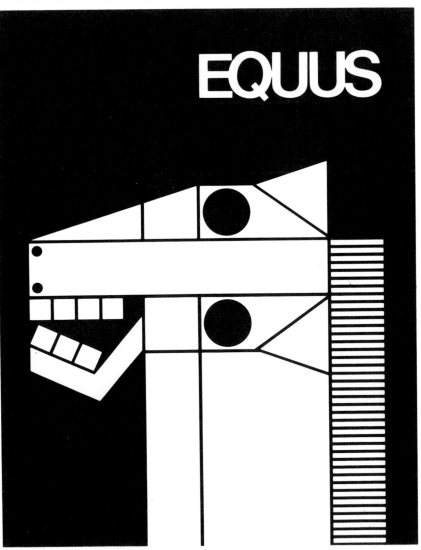

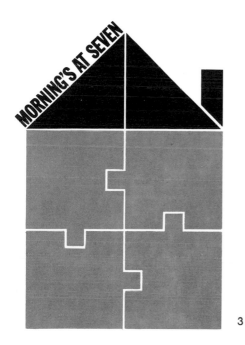

Designer: Gilbert Lesser

1
_____
Equus
Agency: Blaine-Thompson Advertising

2
_____
The Suicide
Agency: Ash/LeDonne, Inc.

3
_____
Morning's at Seven
Agency: Serino, Coyne & Nappi, Inc.

4
_____
Frankenstein
Agency: Ash/LeDonne, Inc.

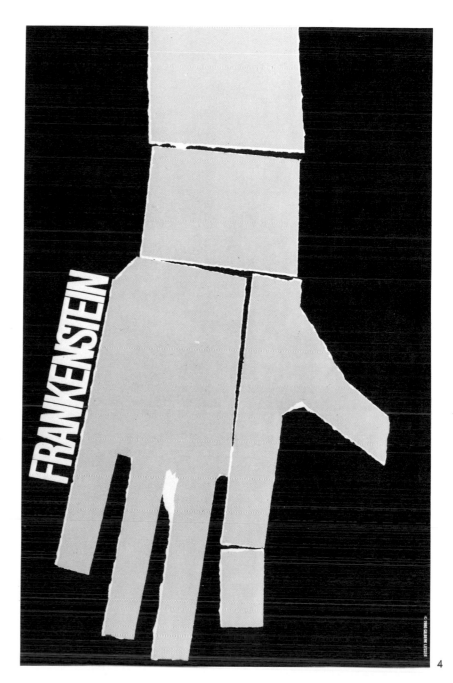

Lesser's unpublished designs for *Amadeus* richly demonstrate the range of variation possible on a single motif; in this case, the mask imagery from the second act of Peter Shaffer's dramatic exploration of the real or imagined destruction of Wolfgang Amadeus Mozart by a mediocre rival, Antonio Salieri. Lesser's final concept (plate 3) is based on an actual 18th century silhouette of Salieri, made menacing by Lesser's distinctive penchant for torn paper.

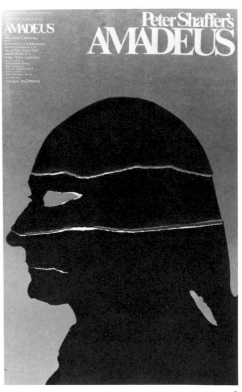

3

2

Designer: Gilbert Lesser

1, 2, 3
Unpublished designs for *Amadeus*

4
The American Clock
Agency: Serino, Coyne & Nappi, Inc.

5
The Elephant Man
Agency: Serino, Coyne & Nappi, Inc.

5

Posters and Illustration

The creepy cobweb tracery of illustrator Edward Gorey has long been admired by readers of curious, hard-to-find books, but Gorey's largest public has undeniably been won through his visual contributions to the performing arts. His sets and costumes for the enormously successful revival of *Dracula* on Broadway were among the most memorable in recent theatre seasons, and his ongoing work for the New York City Ballet is perhaps the most prominent example of a graphic artist enhancing the public image of a performing arts institution. Gorey designs embellish NYCB posters, totebags, coffee mugs, playing cards, lapel buttons, keychains, and just about anything else that can be dreamed up. Gorey collectibles provide a significant source of earned income for the non-profit ballet, according to the Ballet's gift bar director, Rosalie Lewis.

Gorey himself is a notorious balletomane, and is reported to have seen nearly every performance of the New York City Ballet since 1956. In addition to his stage designs for *Dracula*, he has designed productions of several ballets, including *Swan Lake*, and recently tried his hand at an opera, *Don Giovanni*. He divides his time between Cape Cod (summer) and New York (winter), where he can be seen haunting Lincoln Center in massive fur coats and tennis shoes. Obviously a unique talent and personality, Gorey once told a *People* magazine interviewer, "I've been totally eccentric for an awful long time."

Edward Gorey

I SAW DRACULA!

1

78

Designer: Edward Gorey

1
_____
Dracula
Teeshirt design

2
_____
Trinity Square Repertory Theatre
Poster

2

1

2

4

1–5
New York City Ballet
Marketing items
Designer: Edward Gorey

In addition to many other distinctions, Lanford Wilson may be the only Pulitzer Prize-winning playwright who originally aimed to be a graphic designer. "I didn't want to write plays," says the man who ended up writing more than a few, including *The Hot l Baltimore, Talley's Folly* and *Fifth of July.* "I hoped to be a graphic artist. But while I was working at Fuller, Smith and Ross Advertising in Chicago, little snippets of dialogue kept appearing at the margins of my rough layouts. Now I find my writing notebooks filled with ideas for posters. To resolve this schizophrenia I say that I write plays in order to design the posters. I suspect I'm equally inept at both, but I enjoy both enormously. The poster might not sell the play, but it looks great on my wall."

Lanford Wilson

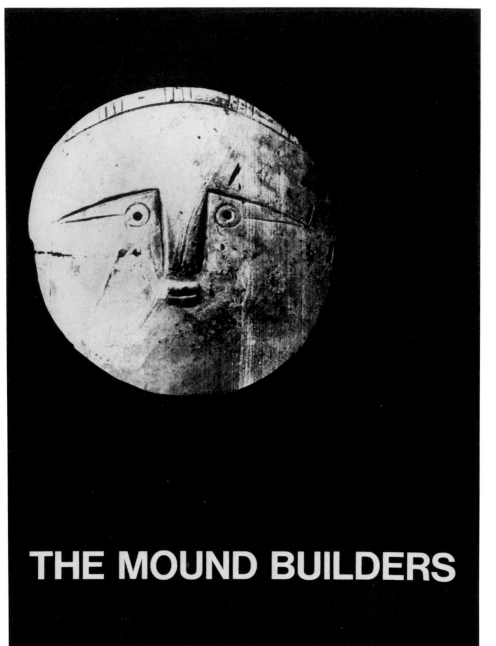

THE MOUND BUILDERS

LANFORD WILSON'S THE MOUND BUILDERS. DIRECTED BY MARSHALL W. MASON. WITH: TANYA BEREZIN / STEPHANIE GORDON / TRISH HAWKINS / JONATHAN HOGAN / LAUREN S. JACOBS JOHN STRASBERG / ROB THIRKIELD.   SET BY JOHN LEE BEATTY   /   LIGHTING BY DENNIS PARICHY COSTUMES BY JENNIFER VON MAYRHAUSER / SOUND & VISUALS BY CHUCK LONDON & GEORGE HANSEN PHOTOS BY ROB THIRKIELD & JERRY ROBERTS   /   ONE MONTH ONLY: PREVIEWS BEGIN JANUARY 29 OPENS FEBRUARY 2   /   TUESDAY THRU FRIDAY 8 PM   /   SATURDAY 7 PM & 10 PM   /   SUNDAY 3 PM CIRCLE REPERTORY COMPANY   99 SEVENTH AVENUE SOUTH ON SHERIDAN SQUARE   924-7100

1

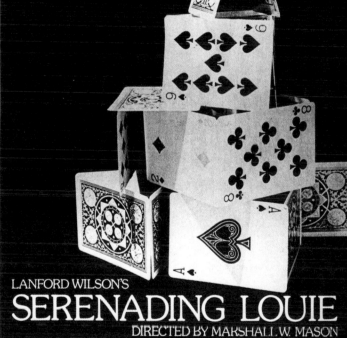

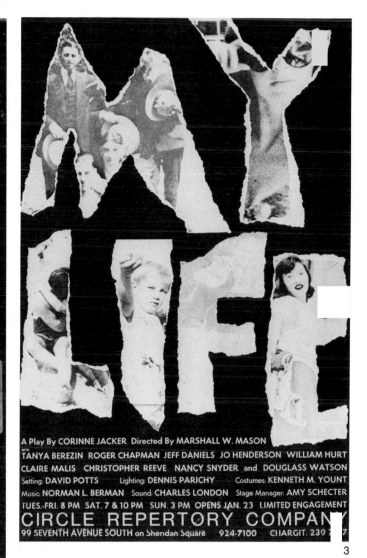

Circle Repertory Company

Circle Repertory Company

1
_____
Designer: Lanford Wilson

2
_____
Concept: Lanford Wilson
Execution: Daniel Irvine

3
_____
Designers: Lanford Wilson and Daniel Irvine

The display advertisement is a form closely related to the poster, but one with its own special challenges as well. To be effective, a display ad, like the poster, must catch and rivet attention, but it usually has none of the poster's advantages of size, color and impact.

Space is usually tight, and often a great deal of information must be compressed into a small area. Moreover, the performing arts display ad is fighting for the reader's attention with surrounding clutter of other entertainment ads and listings. The artwork and typography must be able to vie successfully in this noisy "bulletin board" environment. Strong areas of light and dark coupled with bold typography are always good bets in the display ad arena; fine halftones and low-contrast photography will inevitably be reduced to gray smears by the vagaries of newspaper reproduction.

Display advertisments are used by performing arts groups primarily to attract single-ticket patrons, as well as to provide timely information on performance schedules, box office telephone, etc. As newspaper advertising rates become more expensive, creative directors are increasingly challenged to develop maximum design impact with a minimum of words and visuals.

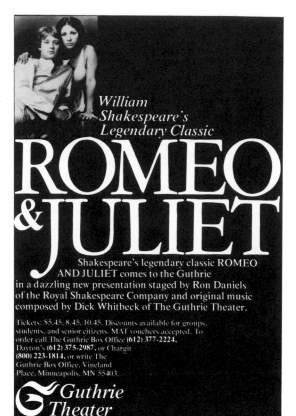

1

2

3

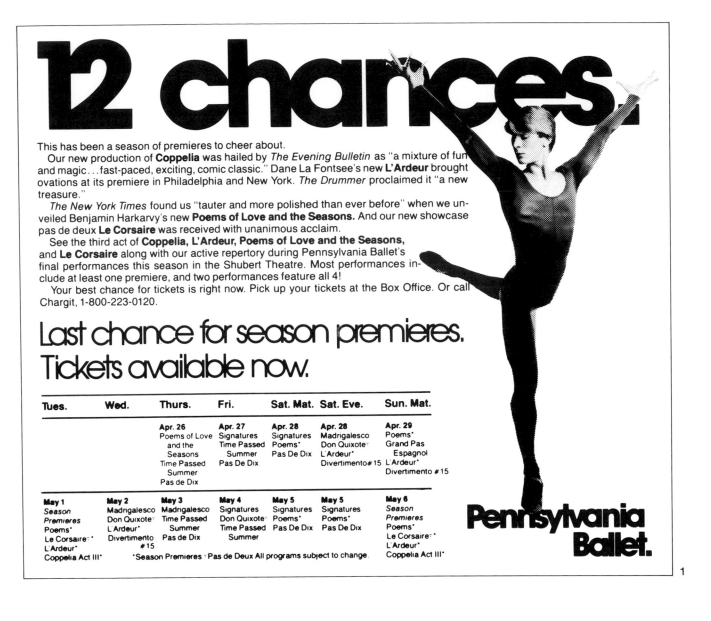

12 chances.

This has been a season of premieres to cheer about.

Our new production of **Coppelia** was hailed by *The Evening Bulletin* as "a mixture of fun and magic...fast-paced, exciting, comic classic." Dane La Fontsee's new **L'Ardeur** brought ovations at its premiere in Philadelphia and New York. *The Drummer* proclaimed it "a new treasure."

The New York Times found us "tauter and more polished than ever before" when we unveiled Benjamin Harkarvy's new **Poems of Love and the Seasons.** And our new showcase pas de deux **Le Corsaire** was received with unanimous acclaim.

See the third act of **Coppelia, L'Ardeur, Poems of Love and the Seasons,** and **Le Corsaire** along with our active repertory during Pennsylvania Ballet's final performances this season in the Shubert Theatre. Most performances include at least one premiere, and two performances feature all 4!

Your best chance for tickets is right now. Pick up your tickets at the Box Office. Or call Chargit, 1-800-223-0120.

Last chance for season premieres. Tickets available now.

Tues.	Wed.	Thurs.	Fri.	Sat. Mat.	Sat. Eve.	Sun. Mat.
		Apr. 26 Poems of Love and the Seasons Time Passed Summer Pas de Dix	**Apr. 27** Signatures Time Passed Summer Pas De Dix	**Apr. 28** Signatures Poems* Pas De Dix	**Apr. 28** Madrigalesco Don Quixote⁻ L'Ardeur* Divertimento# 15	**Apr. 29** Poems* Grand Pas Espagnol L'Ardeur* Divertimento # 15
May 1 Season Premieres Poems* Le Corsaire⁻* L'Ardeur* Coppelia Act III*	**May 2** Madrigalesco Don Quixote⁻ L'Ardeur* Divertimento # 15	**May 3** Madrigalesco Time Passed Summer Pas de Dix	**May 4** Signatures Don Quixote⁻ Time Passed Summer	**May 5** Signatures Poems* Pas De Dix	**May 5** Signatures Poems* Pas De Dix	**May 6** Season Premieres Poems* Le Corsaire⁻* L'Ardeur* Coppelia Act III*

*Season Premieres ⁻Pas de Deux All programs subject to change.

Pennsylvania Ballet.

1

1-3

Pennsylvania Ballet
Art Director: Gene Massimo
Creative Director: Craig Palmer
Design Firm: Palmer Communications

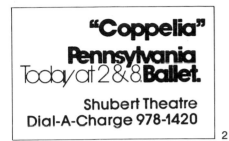
Contrary to popular mythology, it is frequently possible to include a great density of information in the limited space of a display advertisement without sacrificing design integrity. This ad campaign by Palmer Communications for the Pennsylvania Ballet provides an excellent demonstration.

That the principles of good display advertising can be successfully implemented in such larger-than-life circumstances as the highway billboard is clearly illustrated by these outdoor advertisements for the Guthrie Theater.

1

2

1–4
Guthrie Theater
Design: Markgraf & Wells Advertising

3

4

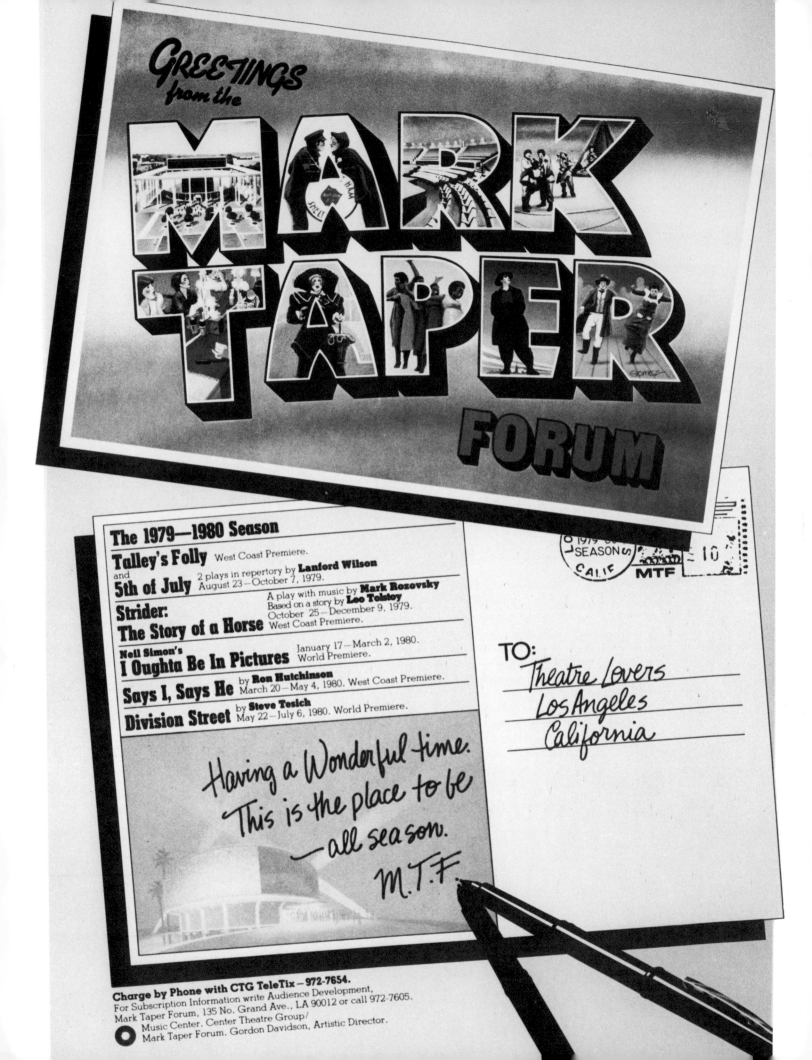

GREETINGS from the MARK TAPER FORUM

The 1979—1980 Season

Talley's Folly West Coast Premiere.
and
5th of July 2 plays in repertory by **Lanford Wilson**
August 23—October 7, 1979.

Strider: A play with music by **Mark Rozovsky**
Based on a story by **Leo Tolstoy**
October 25—December 9, 1979.
The Story of a Horse West Coast Premiere.

Neil Simon's January 17—March 2, 1980.
I Oughta Be In Pictures World Premiere.

Says I, Says He by **Ron Hutchinson**
March 20—May 4, 1980. West Coast Premiere.

Division Street by **Steve Tesich**
May 22—July 6, 1980. World Premiere.

*Having a Wonderful time.
This is the place to be
— all season.
M.T.F.*

TO:
Theatre Lovers
Los Angeles
California

Charge by Phone with CTG TeleTix — 972-7654.
For Subscription Information write Audience Development,
Mark Taper Forum, 135 No. Grand Ave., LA 90012 or call 972-7605.
Music Center. Center Theatre Group/
Mark Taper Forum. Gordon Davidson, Artistic Director.

Direct Mail

Effective direct mail promotion is the foundation of marketing in the performing arts, and direct mail materials offer their most challenging opportunities to graphic designers and marketing specialists. Unlike posters, which allow the designer almost unlimited latitude in form and execution, the direct mail piece is a more disciplined exercise. To succeed, it must create a point-of-purchase—that is its *raison d'être*. There is no room here for self-indulgence on the designer's part; it is the direct mail piece that most assuredly tests the skills and ingenuity of the graphic designer as a *communicator.*

The nature of communications and advertising graphics has changed radically in the last two decades. Now more than ever nonprofit groups must compete for the consumer's attention one-on-one with advertising that in itself has become a minor form of entertainment. If institutional companies cannot afford to enter the arena of broadcast promotion—what Robert Hughes in *The Shock of the New* calls "the electronic blizzard" —then they must attempt at least to find an equivalent imagistic potency in print.

The physical presentation of promotional campaigns is an area that is frequently neglected; indeed, there is often a tendency for busy subscription managers to take their promotional inspiration from the brochures of other institutions rather than basing them on their own specific needs and audience profile. But as institutional budgets and the public's disposable income are increasingly restricted, audience research will become more important in the planning, design and execution of subscription campaigns.

The designer can be central to the marketing process. If, for instance, research has shown that the experience of *theatre-going* is more important to your audience than the impact of particular plays, what kinds of words and images might reinforce such an appeal? Motivational research is a powerful tool for both the marketing director and designer, and can no longer be excluded from an effective campaign.

While there may not be a direct correlation between sales and good graphics *per se*, there is certainly a connection between the success of a campaign and the amount of thought invested in it. In this context, employed dynamically as a conceptual tool, graphic design can undeniably complement, underscore and enhance the effectiveness of any promotional effort.

The techniques and appeals developed by nonprofit groups over the last twenty years must obviously continue to be refined to meet the challenge of new audiences; the visual and presentational aspects in particular need to catch up with the marketing realities of the 1980s.

1

Mark Taper Forum
Illustrator: Ignacio Gomez
Art Director: Elizabeth Kooker

Atlanta's Alliance Theatre Company has mounted several successful subscription campaigns around humorous images of "audience members," creating an effective promotional continuity from season to season and also making a positive statement about the importance of the audience to the institution. Public relations director Mark Arnold comments:

"As we were completing one of our most popular seasons, a line to the box office seemed an ideal visual. 'Don't Stand for It' became the theme of our subscription campaign, with copy evolving naturally from the slogan, expressing in sharp simple terms the many benefits of subscribing (Don't Stand for Sold Out, Don't Stand for Last Row, Don't Stand for High Prices, Don't Stand for No Exchanges, Don't Stand for Less than Alliance).

"Of course the season itself is the primary sell, and by creating bright graphic identities for each of the productions, we hope to generate excitement for the full season. We plan to use the design for posters as each production evolves.

"The models you see are strictly volunteers, culled from the Alliance staff, friends and actors. Ten set-ups in all were used to create the line, all done in a photographer's studio except for the shot of the box office. The order was determined after the photos were processed, and certain effects were created through stripping (the hippie next to the guitar player was actually from a different shot altogether). Each set-up included four to five people. A total of 200,000 brochures were printed."

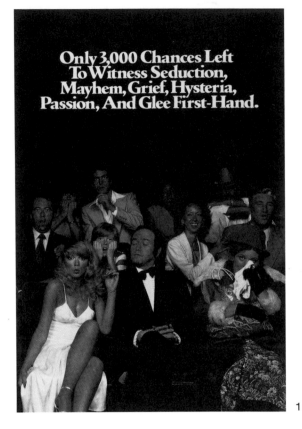

1

2

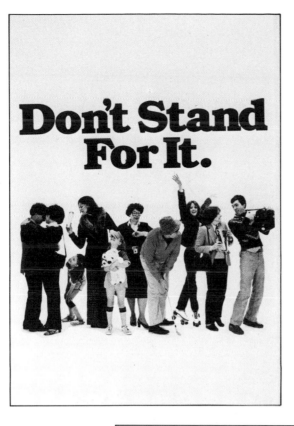

Alliance Theatre Company

1
Creative Direction: Flemister &
Burkhardt, Inc.
Photographer: Jamie Cook

2
Creative Direction: Ron Burkhardt and
Ed Martell
Photographer: Arington Hendley

3
Designers: Larry Paulsen and Sherry
Paulsen
Creative Director: Mark Arnold
Photographer: Jamie Cook

3

"The look and quality of the promotional material bears an inescapable relationship to the reader's impression of the work being promoted," says William E. Power, graphic designer for Manhattan Theatre Club, Circle Repertory Company and other New York-based arts groups.

"For small companies in a city like New York, the audience market is finite, especially in the present economy. It's important that arts groups identify themselves at the same time they identify their markets. Identify *and* differentiate. Obviously, in a competitive market, a dozen companies putting forth the same kinds of promotional materials—the same kinds of promotional appeal, the same kinds of copy and slogans—are going to cancel each other out.

"It's important to target the appeal," says Power. "Before I design a piece, I want to know everything I can about the audience members themselves—their ages, their incomes, what image the theatre has in their marketplace, and finally, the image they have of themselves.

"I think that a theatre's graphics can look highly professional and still be produced economically. I don't see any reason, for instance, for a designer to use more than two colors on a brochure—anything else is a waste of money. Whenever possible, paper buys should be made in bulk and in advance of anticipated needs. Paper prices go up like oil, except that you don't hear about it on the nightly news. A systematic approach to design, with coordinated formats and anticipated production requirements, makes advance planning much easier."

1

MANHATTAN THEATRE CLUB

Lynne Meadow, Artistic Director
Barry Grove, Managing Director
321 East 73rd Street
New York, New York 10021

Non-Profit Org.
U.S. Postage
PAID
New York, N.Y.
Permit No. 5908

MANHATTAN THEATRE CLUB

Lynne Meadow, Artistic Director   321 East 73rd Street
Barry Grove, Managing Director   New York, New York 10021

1

Manhattan Theatre Club
Designer: William E. Power

Symphony orchestras offer some of the most challenging assignments to brochure designers because of the length and complexity of orchestral subscription programs—detailed and often overlapping "series" featuring dozens of works, composers and/or guest artists. In order to avoid deadly grey columns of type, many designers find the solution to the problem within the problem itself, by emphasizing *typography* as a major design element, as seen in William Wondriska's stunningly effective piece for the Hartford Symphony.

Not surprisingly, most of the routine problems of brochure design—presentation of play descriptions, seating charts, repertory calendars, etc.—are most successful when presented without embellishment. The most striking effects are usually achieved through selective *emphasis*, not ornamentation.

1

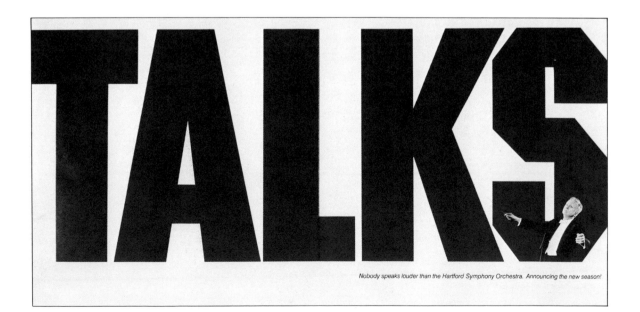

Nobody speaks louder than the Hartford Symphony Orchestra. Announcing the new season!

1

Hartford Symphony Orchestra
Designer: William Wondriska

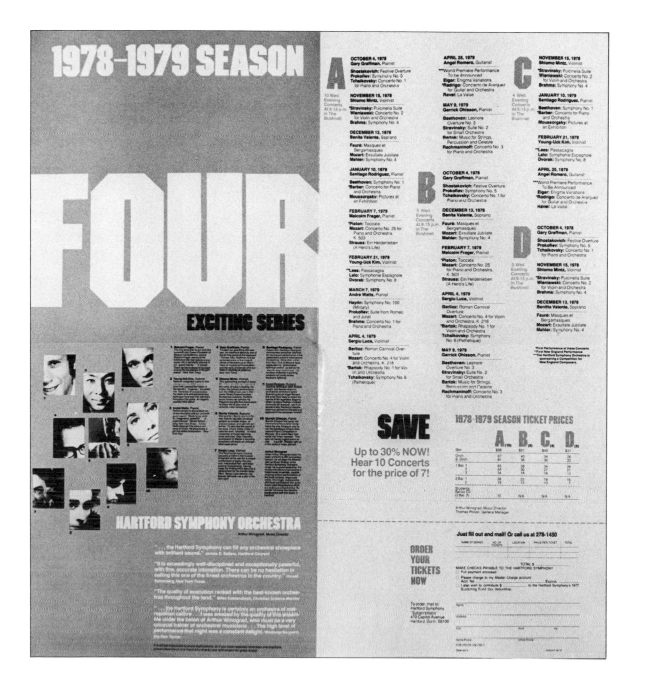

1

Seattle Repertory Theatre
Designer: Ellen Ziegler
Illustrator: Fred Hilliard

AND IT'S STILL
GOING STRONG.

Except now, instead of just a theatre,
The Rep is a Tradition.

And that's not the kind of thing that
happens overnight. Or without good
reason.

From the beginning, we were the
most exciting and innovative theatre i

1

EIGHTEEN YEARS AGO, THE ENTERTAINMENT-
STARVED CITIZENS OF SEATTLE GOT
THE THEATRE THEY WANTED.

attle. That part was easy—we had a hole city behind us, helping us along, couraging us.

hen we matured, until The Rep became Seattle what the Mark Taper Forum is Los Angeles, A.C.T. is to San Francisco, The Guthrie to Minneapolis and e Washington Arena to the nation's apitol.

It took awhile, but we did it. And we did it with flair.

It's pretty heady stuff being a Tradition. And it's a responsibility, too.

That's why The Rep hired artistic directors John Hirsch and Daniel Sullivan. These exceptional men understand creative excellence.

But more than that, they believe in Seattle, in the people who live here, and in The Rep. And they're committed to bringing their audiences brilliant theatre. The kind of theatre you'd expect from a Tradition.

On opening night, October 22, 1980, The Rep will begin its 18th year. To celebrate our Coming of Age, we've planned our most captivating season yet.

The glitter, the wonder, the laughter and tears—the fascination of live theatre at its very best—are all awaiting you at The Seattle Rep. An Entertainment Tradition.

Be they simple or startling, the outside panels of a direct mail piece must be striking enough to prompt the recipient to look inside—otherwise the piece has failed utterly. As shown here, the approach may be as varied as a bold typographical command, an attractive illustration, or self-assured use of white space. Whatever the technique, the maximum impact is achieved when the outside of the mailer stands out prominently from the mailbox's daily plethora of utility bills, magazines and catalogs. Perhaps the worst thing a designer can do is to create a brochure that virtually reads as "just another piece of junk mail."

1

2

1
Opera Theatre of St. Louis
Designer: Jan Boleto

2
San Diego Symphony
Designer: Dennis Gillaspy

3
Harold Clurman Theatre
Designers: Diana Graham and
Aubrey Balkind
Design Firm: Gips & Balkind &
Associates, Inc.

THE HAROLD CLURMAN THE★TRE

1980-81 SUPER SEASON

SUBSCRIBE NOW AND SAVE!

Dear Friend,

It has been a truly exciting experience preparing the 1980-81 season at the Harold Clurman Theatre and we can hardly wait to share our upcoming program with you. We are about to launch our most successful season yet, offering subscribers a variety of plays, films, experimental workshop theatre all topped by "weekend cabarets".

We would like our new and old subscribers to know that this season's program reflects the continuing aim and dedication of the Harold Clurman Theatre: the production of the best **Plays** with the development of new works and the revitalization of rare existing works both foreign and American, directed in the most imaginative and professional way, and acted by a company of expert actors.

Our **Workshop** series, *New Works "Upstairs"* is a program where both experienced and new playwrights and directors can experiment in the informal studio-theatre

atmosphere offering the audience the opportunity to be part of the creative process as new works evolve.

The **Film Program** at the Clurman Theatre is designed to serve foreign and domestic films of artistic value that would not otherwise be shown in a commercial theatre.

This season, the Clurman Theatre takes great delight in introducing evenings of **Cabaret**. Bobby LuPone, star of A Chorus Line, has joined us as the Program Director. These evenings of cabaret promise to offer new musical material performed by great singing and dancing talent.

Superior theatre in the final analysis is dependent on you, the audience. Harold Clurman and I hope you will join us and share in an exciting and vital theatrical experience.

Jack Garfein
Jack Garfein
Artistic Director

SAVE!

In our third season we invite you to enjoy three spectacular new theatrical productions, three exhilarating evenings of workshops, two exclusive cinematic premieres, a most unusual series of ten great films and your choice of one of our new Cabaret events.
All for the price of two Broadway shows!

Arthur Miller's
The American Clock
"Arthur Miller is back at the top of his talent. The actors are as fine as the writing."
Frank Rich,
New York Times

"Wholly satisfying experience. The production rivals any production on any stage in this world today."
William Furtwangler,
Charleston News & Courier (Spoleto Festival)

Paul Shyre's
Paris Was Yesterday
"Celeste Holm is impeccable as Janet Flanner in Paris Was Yesterday."
Clive Barnes,
New York Post

PLAYS

A Chekhov Sketchbook
The American premiere of an extraordinary new production dramatized by Luba Kadison and starring Joseph Buloff. Directed by Tony Giordano.

Lakeboat
The New York premiere of a new play by David Mamet, prize-winning author of *American Buffalo* and *A Life in the Theatre*.

A third play will be chosen from:

QED, a new comedy by Ben Starr, directed by Brian Murray.
Miss Julie by August Strindberg. A new translation by Evert Sprinchorn and directed by Jack Garfein.

Arthur Miller's
The Price
"The Price is Arthur Miller's best. This is the definitive production of this play. Every second and much beyond is magnificent."
Clive Barnes,
New York Post

"All Buloff should be doing is being a national treasure."
Ted Kalem,
Time Magazine

FILMS

Two Film Premieres!
In the tradition of last season's *The Apple Game, Death of a Bureaucrat, The Wrong Move* and *California Reich*, The Harold Clurman Theatre presents two stunning new films. Audiences have been delighted with the high quality and originality of our film "finds."

Film Series
Your subscription includes tickets to all ten of the movies in our highly acclaimed film series. Last year, we presented *Road Movies, Central Casting* and *Shakespeare on Film*. This year we will choose another outstanding selection of films for your enjoyment.

Road Movies
"The Road Movie series at the Clurman Theatre is a wide ranging and eclectic series of movie fare."
Stephen Harvey,
New York Times

The Apple Game
"The Apple Game is one of Czechoslovakia's first movies to earn an honest-to-goodness Oscar nomination. It is a charming and wonderfully funny film."
Roger Angell,
New Yorker Magazine

The Wrong Move
"Wim Wenders' The Wrong Move is astonishingly lovely."
Vincent Canby,
New York Times

WORKSHOPS

Two Character Play by Tennessee Williams. Directed by Alfred Ryder with Olive Deering and Mr. Ryder.

White Jazz. An open rehearsal of Michael Moriarty's one-man musical will be part of our season depending on Mr. Moriarty's availability.

An Ounce of Prevention by Hal Corley. Directed by Larry Harbison.

"Upstairs" workshops allow you to participate as a new play evolves and to experience the exciting, intimate studio-theatre atmosphere at the Clurman Theatre. You will also have the chance to meet the actors, playwrights and directors.

The California Reich
"A rare film. The Clurman Theatre is the most important new theatre of intent live in the city."
Tom Allen,
Village Voice

Mayo Simon's
These Men
"A charged play about two women."
Clive Barnes,
New York Post

"The film is wonderful and Jill Larson is marvelous."
Richard Sheppard,
New York Times

CABARET

Dream Time
Debbie Shapiro stars in a new show with lyrics by Alfred Uhry, music by Robert Waldman. Bobby Lupone will direct and choreograph.

Other Cabarets
A second cabaret will be chosen from:

An evening filled with Country and Western music.

A show about two women exploring sex and the rock culture.

A nostalgic trip to the music of the thirties.

A look at tap—a unique form of American dance.

Eugene Ionesco's
The Lesson
"A real Off-B'way event. Guided by Jack Garfein's seasoned direction, a triumph, getting a 15st time out off to a flying start with a most winning staff."
Bob Lay,
WABC-TV, New York

SAVE 50%

It should be apparent by this time that there is often no sharp distinction between an effective poster design and an effective design for a brochure, mailing piece or advertisement, other than the considerations of physical size and impact. In his coordinated subscription brochure and poster for San Francisco's Magic Theatre, designer James McCaffry employs a startling, up-to-the-minute visual approach to match the theatre's reputation as a front-runner of the avant-garde.

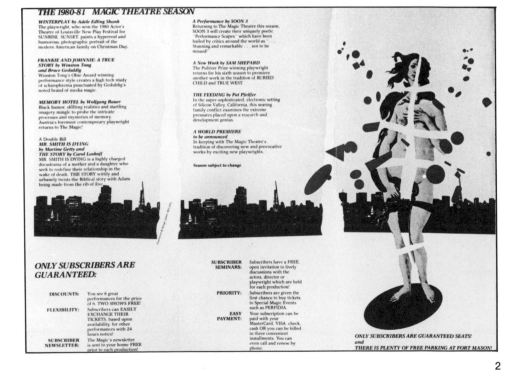

1

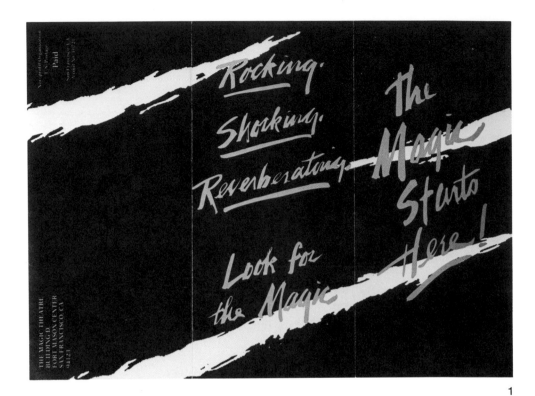

2

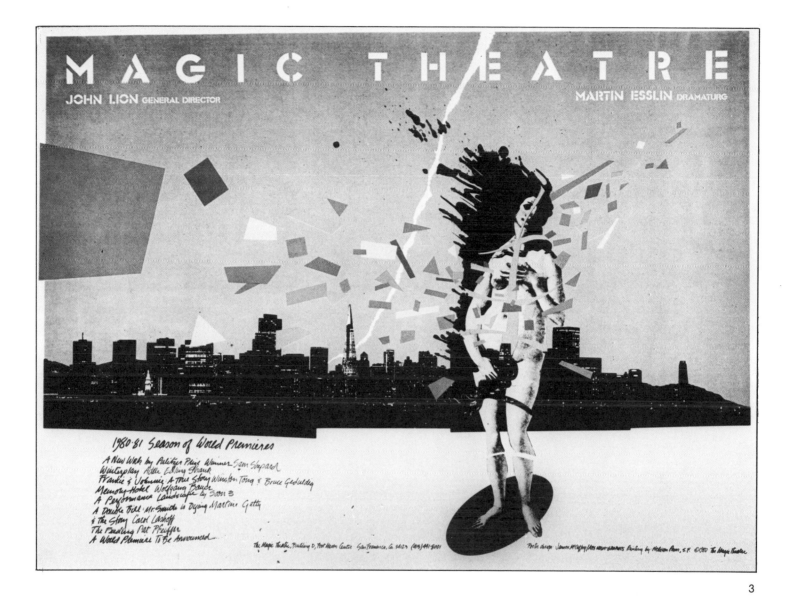

1
Magic Theatre
Designer: James McCaffry

Clark Kellogg, a transplanted Californian currently completing his training as an architect in New York, began designing flyers and posters for the performing arts as a favor to his neighbor, dance soloist Daniel Nagrin. He has since devised a variety of striking pieces for Off-Off Broadway productions, most of which have been executed on extremely limited budgets. Working simply in line, developing high contrast images that can be reduced to one-column newspaper ads or exploded as posters, he effectively achieves visual as well as financial economy.

He likes to be involved early on in the development of a promotional piece, but sometimes solutions need to be found on the spur of the moment. For a cabaret performance by singer Donna Emmanuel, Kellogg designed a system of flyers and table cards that were reproduced on an office copying machine, with a spot of color added by hand with a felt pen. The results rivaled the quality of a two-color offset job.

Kellogg enjoys the creative challenges and doesn't mind budgetary restrictions. (However, he is quick to point out that he does not attempt to make his living from graphic design.) In order to derive the greatest satisfaction despite technical or financial constraints, he feels that "it's important to recognize the project for what it *is*, and not what I might want it to be."

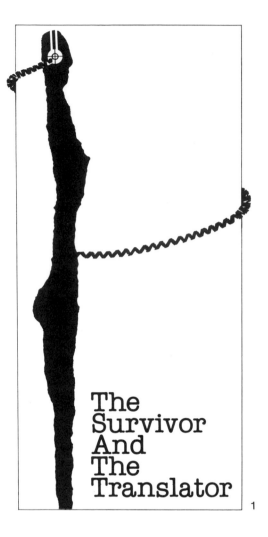

1

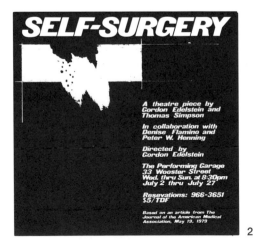

2

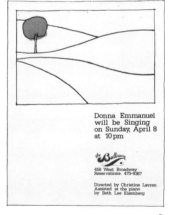

3

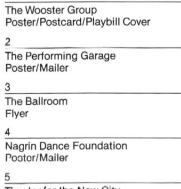

Daniel Nagrin performs 'Jacaranda (a dance)' written for him by Sam Shepard

Choreography: Daniel Nagrin
Sets and Costumes: Sally Ann Parsons
Lights: Gary Harris

The Riverside Dance Festival
The Theatre of the Riverside Church
490 Riverside Dr. (at 120 St.)

Wednesday, May 16   8 pm
Friday, May 18   8 pm
Sunday, May 20   8 pm

Tickets $4.50
$3.50 Students, $3.00 Senior Citizens
or TDF + $1.00
Reservations 864-2929

This work was made possible with a grant from the
Creative Artists Public Service Program and with
public funds from the New York State Council on the Arts.

© 1979, Clark Kellogg

4

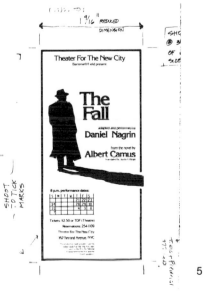

5

In the outer realms of avant-garde theatre, even the design and execution of a mailing piece can become an integral part of the artistic event. Such was the case with Rudy Kocevar's *Art Wars*, presented in December 1980 at La Mama E.T.C. in New York City.

In addition to the performance itself, the bulk mailing for *Art Wars* was conceived and executed by Kocevar as an act of conceptual art. Five thousand flyers, each an original within a progression of multiples, were mailed at random to Theatre Development Fund subscribers. Mechanical processes were utilized in the first three sets: offset reproduction, hole punches and rubber stamps. The holes functioned to reinforce the flyer's existence in three-dimensional space, while the stamp introduced color. With the freely drawn marker application, a process of individuation was established, which was continued with spray paint. The conceptual significance of each set within the progression determined the number of pieces mailed from that set.

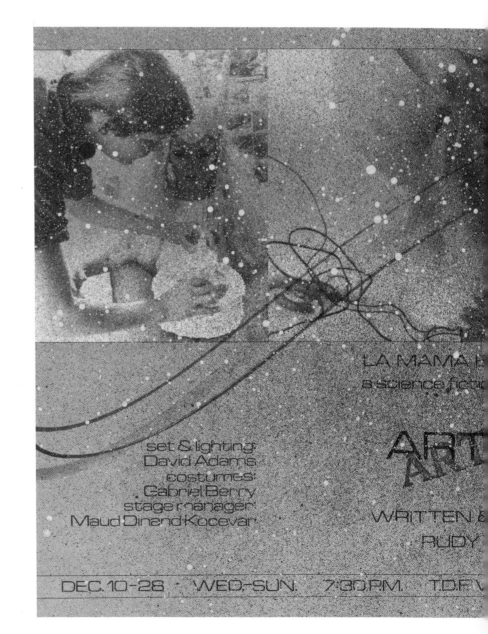

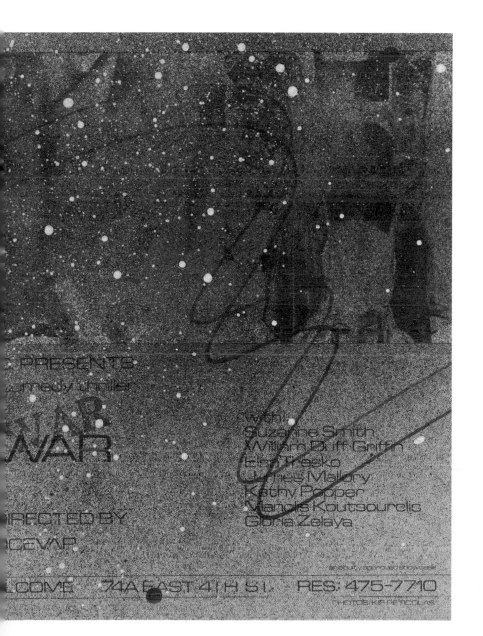

1
La Mama E.T.C.
Designer: Rudy Kocevar
Photographer: Kip Peticolas

The sorting rooms of the New York City post office are routinely swamped with inexpensively produced flyers, mailers and postcards publicizing the performing arts, in volumes that probably rival the overall postal traffic of many small towns. Often, a surprising amount of ingenuity is apparent in the creation of these "throwaway" pieces, which frequently employ the simplest line drawings to stunning effect.

1

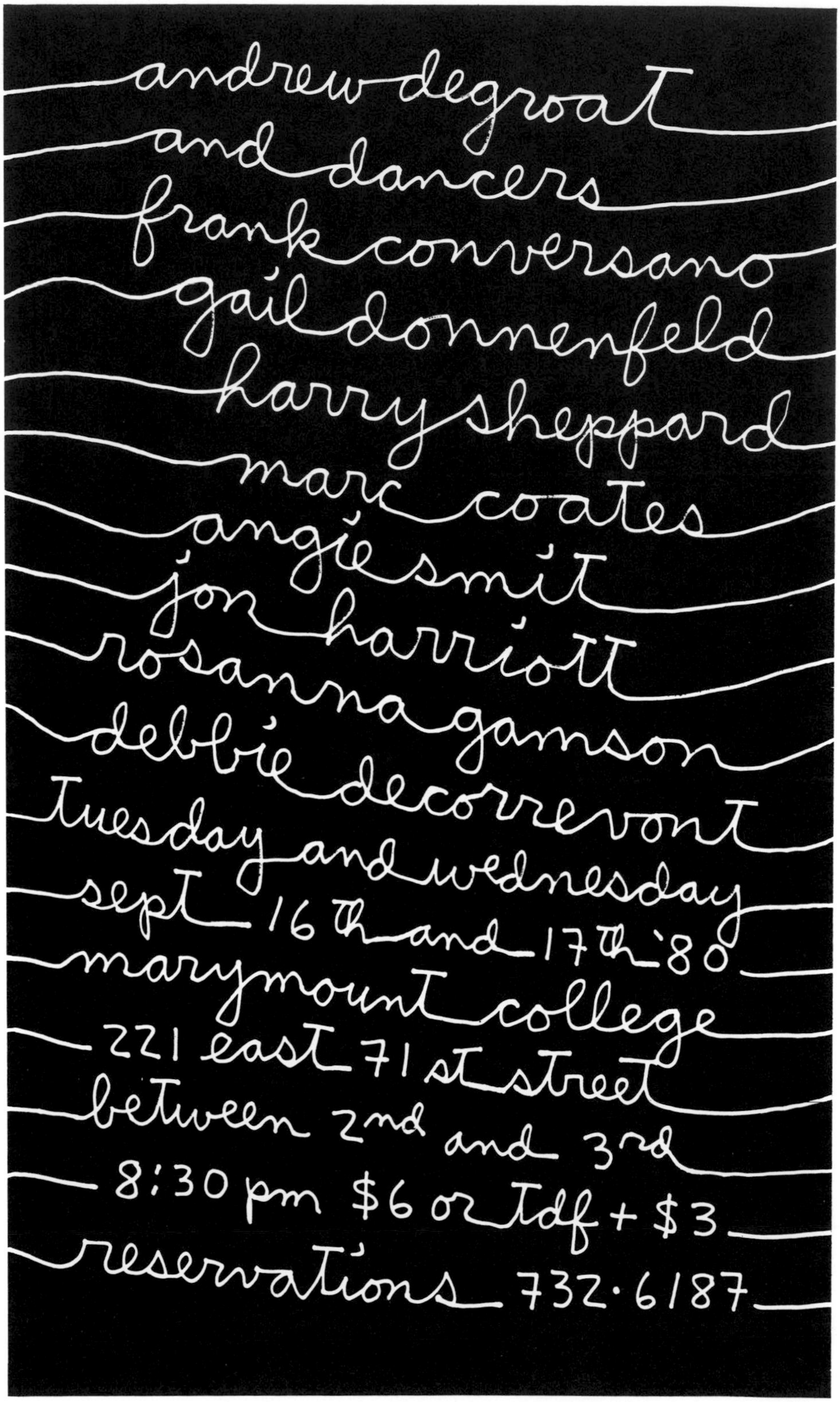

andrew degroat
and dancers
frank conversano
gail donnenfeld
harry sheppard
marc coates
angie smit
jon harriott
rosanna gamson
debbie decorrevont
tuesday and wednesday
sept 16th and 17th '80
marymount college
221 east 71st street
between 2nd and 3rd
8:30 pm $6 or Tdf + $3
reservations 732·6187

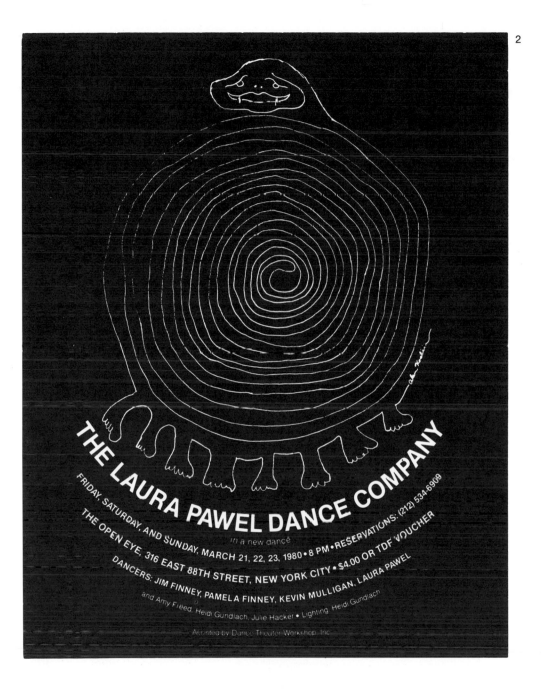

1
_____
Andrew deGroat and Dancers
Designer: Andrew deGroat

2
_____
Laura Pawel Dance Company
Design: Linda Briggs

music center   unified fund

1981

Fund-Raising and Institutional Promotion

Like direct mail promotions, fund-raising campaigns are a form of persuasive advertising that lend themselves well to exciting graphic interpretation. Unlike direct mail subscription sales, the fund raising appeal emphasizes an institution's services, achievements and standing in the community, rather than the convenience and economy of purchasing a season ticket. While fund-raising pieces open up the *design* possibilities more broadly than subscription promotions, it is important to remember that it is harder to solicit a contribution than it is to sell a ticket.

Fund-raising materials fall into two general categories—the individual donor solicitation, usually a small printed brochure accompanied by a form appeal letter and return envelope, and the institutional promotion piece, often lavishly illustrated and used to solicit large contributions from the business community. The appeal letter and brochure are most closely related to subscription materials in tone and presentation; a slogan, followed by terse copy outlining the financial realities of nonprofit theatre, dance or music. The approach can range from the whimsical to the unabashedly attention-getting.

The institutional piece, on the other hand, tends to be less aggressive and more concerned with a dignified yet persuasive reflection of a company's activities and achievements. This appeal is more leisurely and oblique; the point being to establish the credibility and prestige of the organization, to outline its accomplishments and to reflect its artistic stance. As these pieces are often created to promote large capital or endowment fund drives, there is often a substantial budget for their preparation, design and printing.

Fund-raising materials must encapsulate a great deal of material without losing momentum. A good design helps to clarify and accentuate essential information. Expressive copywriting, well-chosen type faces and first-rate photography are especially important. The photography in particular should strive to recreate the special energy of live performance.

Obviously, the company that takes care in the production of its ongoing publications—programs, magazines, annual reports, etc., can create its own attractive fund-raising package without incurring the expense of an additional piece. In fact, institutions might even consider prorating part of their regular design and printing expenses as a fund-raising expense, if they utilize their publications in this way. (For more detailed discussion of publications and photography, see the following chapters.)

Fund-raising and institutional promotion materials make particularly stimulating design assignments in that they require an accurate distillation of an institution's aesthetic concerns, as well as its practical aims and achievements. The designer's role here is more subtle and interpretative than in the execution of a splashy poster graphic, more akin to the job of an editorial art director. But fund-raising materials allow perhaps the greatest opportunity for an institution to *directly* express its philosophy and reflect its art.

1
Los Angeles Music Center
Unified Fund Drive
Illustrator David Hockney
Design Firm: James Cross Design Office Inc.

Jim Feldman

SALLY COONEY

Jim Feldman, a specialist in the design of fund-raising and direct-mail materials for New York's larger nonprofit groups, was a finalist in the Corporate Print category at last year's CLIO Awards (the Oscars of the advertising world) for his imaginative joint presentation for the Murray Louis and Nikolais dance companies (right). He also demonstrates a keen perception of the working relationships between graphic designers and arts institutions:

"When I first started to work for the New York City Ballet, I took advantage of the class NYCB offers its staff. It gave me the opportunity to understand position and movement first-hand, and also sensitized my eye to what could make dance move on paper. Seeing a lot of dance also makes it much easier to research thousands of photos and

then pull ten or fifteen which effectively represent the art form. The press office at NYCB has been very helpful at showing me what is *right* in ballet, when a knee is bent or a foot is crooked. They have an extremely well-organized archive containing an enormous amount of visual information.

"Too often, companies keep the visual record only haphazardly. Sometimes there is much information and little organization. Photos are scattered to the four winds, with photographers who have moved to the West Coast, or in libraries, private collections, or stuck in drawers and cartons. Recently, however, there is a different attitude, and people are treating this area much more professionally.

"One of my fears as a designer is of having approval power given to too many people, and thereby

never getting any approval. Arts groups have many levels for approval of work—boards of directors, artistic directors, managers, development people, etc. I always try to work with as small a group of people as possible, and try not to be caught between different interests. I now request consideration of this at the outset and it usually works pretty well.

"Lead time is a sticky issue. Some clients come to you at the last minute and ask for complicated, time-consuming jobs. I seldom say no (unless the deadline is completely ridiculous, and instead take the assignment and hope to educate the client. Explaining the design process in terms of mounting a production works well, I find. A lot of people don't know about fitting type, but they do understand about fitting costumes. You have to learn to speak their language."

1

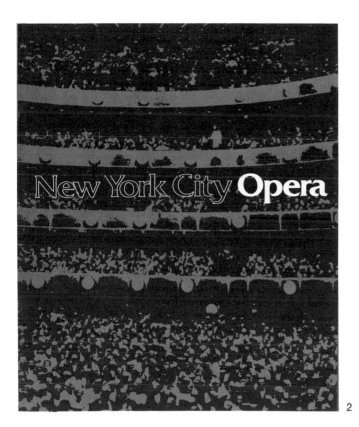

2

Designer: Jim Feldman
Design Firm: Resource Manhattan

Completing the Gesture...

for the New York City Ballet, the gesture is completed with discipline

"*...the subtleties with which steps must be executed preclude fail-safe performance and insure a slightly different one each time round. Occasionally, a critic voices a preference for a non-City Ballet rendition. Given the setup of the home team, though, it can't help but give the most authentic reading. Every night, Balanchine watches it dance from the wings of the stage; every afternoon, he rehearses it; every morning, he conducts a class for it. ...Today, he is the only ballet choreographer who also teaches his dancers, providing a direct route between classroom and stage. 'I teach the technique I learned in Saint Petersburg because only a few dancers know how to clean up their techniques by themselves.' ...a brilliant style that zooms to the top of the top balcony.*"
The New York Times Magazine, May 30, 1976

1
New York City Ballet
Designer: Jim Feldman
Design Firm: Resource Manhattan

Not as a playwright. Or actor. But as a member. A supporter of a powerful force shaping the future of the American theater.

We don't ask you to donate out of blind faith. All we ask is that you read this pamphlet through. Just once. Then you decide if you think the O'Neill Theater Center is worthy of your support.

If you're a theater enthusiast, are now a part of the theater, or are simply concerned about the future of this great American art form, we think the answer will be clear.

Eugene O'Neill Theater Center

505 Great Neck Rd., Waterford, Conn. (0)305 (203) 443-5378
2860 Broadway, New York, N.Y. 10023 (212) 246-1485

the Guthrie Investment

The hail of the trumpets.

...low retreat of ...ounds from the ...ter. It is a call ...a beckoning— ...e begins anew.

...ave become a tradition and a symbol. Since our first theater ...ent our unflagging determination and youthful optimism. ...ds constant vigil and vision.

...contributors, theater-goers, investors—many people must

Introduction

The Guthrie Theater Foundation welcomes lifetime gifts and bequests under a will of all sizes. Bequests play an important role in the well-being of the theater and will continue to do so. However, for those who wish to enjoy during their own lifetimes the personal satisfaction of making a significant contribution to the future of the Guthrie and the additional benefits of income and estate tax savings resulting from their generosity, the theater now offers four life-income gift arrangements: Charitable Remainder Unitrust; Charitable Gift Annuity; the Pooled Income Fund; and Deferred Payment Gift Annuity.

A common feature of these plans is that while making an irrevocable gift of cash, marketable securities, or both, the donor (and/or other beneficiary) continues to enjoy the income for life. Depending on the agreement selected, the life-income arrangement can provide a variable income (thus, a possible hedge against inflation) or fixed, guaranteed payments which will never vary in amount.

Part of every gift will be deductible for Federal income tax purposes as a gift to The Guthrie Theater Foundation. The size of the deduction depends on the initial value of the gift, and the age, sex, number of beneficiaries and the payout percentage. The charitable portion of each gift is deductible up to 30% of the donor's adjusted gross income if the gift is made with long-term appreciated securities, or up to 50% of adjusted gross income if cash is given. Any portion of the charitable contribution not deductible in the year of the gift (because it exceeds the percentage limitation) may be carried forward to generate tax savings for as many as five additional tax years or until it has been exhausted—whichever comes first.

Additionally, the use of appreciated securities for a gift will eliminate, or substantially reduce, capital gains tax. Whether or not capital gains tax will be incurred depends on the form of gift that is made.

The Guthrie Theater Foundation Deferred Giving Programs

3

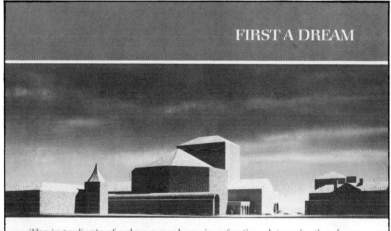

FIRST A DREAM

The ingredients of a dream are here: imagination, determination, love, bricks, mortar and small miracles. And the confidence and contributions of people like you. We are building a place of dreams. The magnificent new Cleveland Play House Theater. A labor of love. And you have a part to play.

4

Fund-Raising and Institutional Promotion

Invest in the making of a great American repertory company

1
BAM Theater Company
Designers: Thomas Dolle and
Ellen Shapiro
Photography: Ken Howard and
Jay Good
Design Firm: Ellen Shapiro Graphic
Design Inc.

2
Theatre Three
Designer/Illustrator: Dean Corbitt

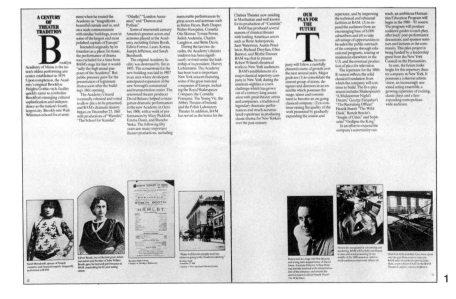

Theatre Three presents

The Case of the Disappearing Dollars

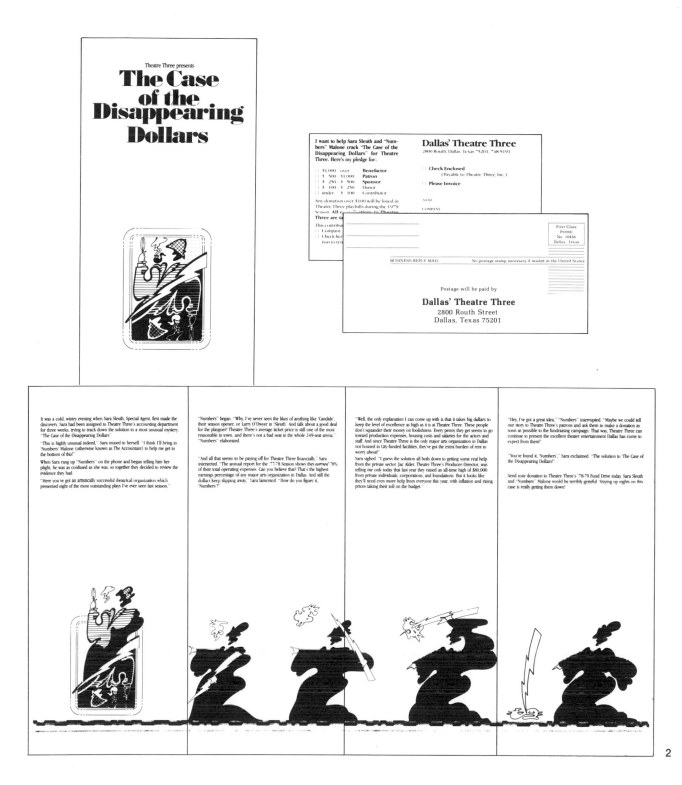

It was a cold, wintry evening when Sara Sleuth, Special Agent, first made the discovery. Sara had been assigned to Theatre Three's accounting department for three weeks, trying to track down the solution to a most unusual mystery, "The Case of the Disappearing Dollars."

"This is highly unusual indeed," Sara mused to herself. "I think I'll bring in 'Numbers' Malone (otherwise known as The Accountant) to help me get to the bottom of this!"

When Sara rang up "Numbers" on the phone and began telling him her plight, he was as confused as she was, so together they decided to review the evidence they had.

"Here you've got an artistically successful theatrical organization which presented eight of the most outstanding plays I've ever seen last season."

"Numbers" began. "Why, I've never seen the likes of anything like 'Candide', their season opener, or Larry O'Dwyer in 'Sleuth'. And talk about a good deal for the playgoer! Theatre Three's average ticket price is still one of the most reasonable in town, and there's not a bad seat in the whole 249-seat arena," "Numbers" elaborated.

"And all that seems to be paying off for Theatre Three financially," Sara interjected. "The annual report for the '77-'78 Season shows they *earned* 78% of their total operating expenses. Can you believe that? That's the highest earnings percentage of any major arts organization in Dallas. And still the dollars keep slipping away," Sara lamented. "How do you figure it, 'Numbers'?"

"Well, the only explanation I can come up with is that it takes big dollars to keep the level of excellence as high as it is at Theatre Three. These people don't squander their money on foolishness. Every penny they get seems to go toward production expenses, housing costs and salaries for the actors and staff. And since Theatre Three is the only major arts organization in Dallas not housed in City-funded facilities, they've got the extra burden of rent to worry about!"

Sara sighed. "I guess the solution all boils down to getting some real help from the private sector. Jac Alder, Theatre Three's Producer-Director, was telling me only today that last year they raised an all-time high of $80,000 from private individuals, corporations, and foundations. But it looks like they'll need even more help from everyone this year, with inflation and rising prices taking their toll on the budget."

"Hey, I've got a great idea," "Numbers" interrupted. "Maybe we could tell our story to Theatre Three's patrons and ask them to make a donation as soon as possible to the fundraising campaign. That way, Theatre Three can continue to present the excellent theater entertainment Dallas has come to expect from them!"

"You've found it, 'Numbers'," Sara exclaimed. "The solution to 'The Case of the Disappearing Dollars!'"

Send your donation to Theatre Three's '78-79 Fund Drive today. Sara Sleuth and "Numbers" Malone would be terribly grateful. Staying up nights on this case is really getting them down!

2

The BAM Theater Company
Audience Magazine

Inside

The Wild Duck

Playbills and Publications

Next to the poster, the playbill or souvenir program is one of the most enduring artifacts of any theatrical production. Graphically distinct from the poster, the program is intended not to entice the reader into the theatre, but to impart information and create a certain effect on the audience before, during and after the actual performance itself. As the only form of graphic design with the potential to *directly* complement performance, the playbill can become a dynamic extension of the artistic event itself. Through judicious use of image and typography, the playbill designer can reinforce a production concept; through incongruous designs, a minor chord of Brechtian alienation may be produced. Unlike direct mail and advertising design, marketing considerations need not predominate.

In recent years, an increasingly common offshoot of the playbill has been the institutional publication, usually mailed to subscribers before the performance. Again, the intention is to put the audience into a receptive mood for the production through the use of detailed production notes, illustrations and other materials. Be they simply newsletters or full-fledged magazines, such publications have a very important function in reinforcing the relationship of the audience and the institution as well as extending the artistic statement of the institution into the mailboxes and living rooms of its constituency.

Still another vital function of the institutional arts publication is to educate and retain audiences. Research has shown that first-time subscribers to cultural programs require "special care and handling" in order to renew their commitment for a second season. It is particularly important to cultivate the subscriber's feeling of connection with the organization. A publication featuring interviews with artists, rehearsal photographs and behind-the-scenes news can be an invaluable tool in strengthening an audience's loyalty and sense of involvement.

1

BAM Theater Company
Designer: Thomas Dolle
Illustrator: David Levine
Creative Directors: Ellen Shapiro and Roger Oliver
Design Firm: Ellen Shapiro Graphic Design Inc.

Unsurpassed for sheer elegance, the programs of the National Theatre of Great Britain maintain a standard of quality for theatrical playbills around the world. In addition to their stylish covers, which are often reproduced as posters, the programs' interiors are laid out with great panache, frequently incorporating rehearsal photographs and historical material. Designers Richard Bird and Michael Mayhew bring to each program impeccable typographical taste, everywhere in evidence, from the photo captions to the cast lists with their distinctive horizontal rules. Respect for the British playbill and the care taken in its preparation are reflected in the fact that audience members are willing to pay 30p each for the privilege of holding and saving these visually dramatic souvenirs.

1

2

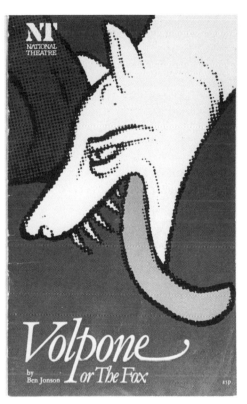

3

4

5

1—5
National Theatre of Great Britain
Designers: Richard Bird and Michael
Mayhew

Doug Johnson's wonderfully ener-
getic illustrations for the programs
of the Chelsea Theater Center demonstrate that the playbill's visual aspect need not stop at the inside
cover. In this coordinated series of
booklets, spot illustrations continued throughout the editorial
matter, and were often as ambitious
and carefully executed as the primary cover designs.

1

2

3

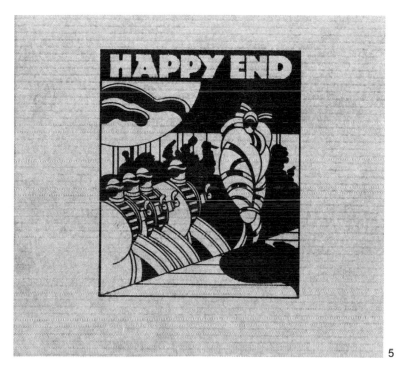

1–6

Chelsea Theater Center
Playbills (with spot illustrations for
The Crazy Locomotive)
Illustrator: Doug Johnson
Design Firm: Performing Dogs

4

5

6

SEATTLE CENTERSTAGE 78-79
SEATTLE REPERTORY THEATRE
THE MASTER BUILDER
NOVEMBER 29 - DECEMBER 23, 1978

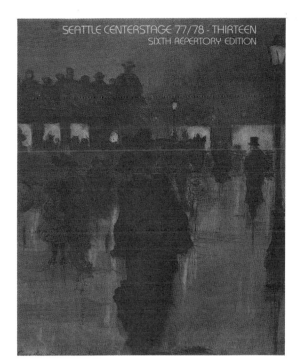

Seattle Repertory Theatre
Design: Bailey Publications

1

Illustrator: Henry Adams, courtesy
Davidson Galleries

2

*The Last Meeting of the Knights of the
White Magnolia*
Illustrator: David Young

3

13 Ruc dc l'amour
Illustrator: Henri Boutet, courtesy
Davidson Galleries

4

The Royal Family
Illustrator: Richard Kirstein-Daiensai,
courtesy Davidson Galleries

5

Anna Christie
Photographer: Greg Gilbert

An important function of the performing arts publication is to prepare the audience for the work they will see on stage. It is therefore no wonder that many organizations have adopted the name *Preview* for their newsletters and magazines. At opposite ends of the country, the Brooklyn Academy of Music and American Conservatory Theatre of San Francisco take boldly divergent graphic approaches.

1
BAM Theatre Company
Design Firm: Ellen Shapiro Graphic
Design, Inc.

2
American Conservatory Theatre
Designer: James McCaffry
Creative Director: Eric Hamburger

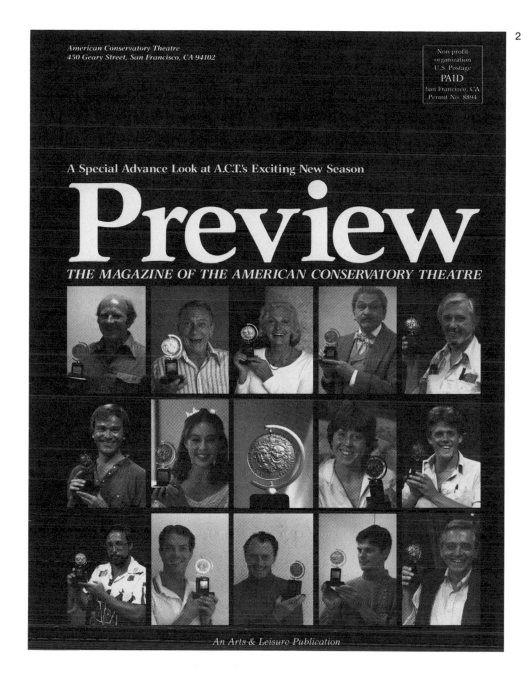

Consistent format is particularly important to the successful publication, be it as simple as the Ohio Ballet's postcard-newsletter or as elaborate as Circle Repertory Company's highly organized three-column grid. Such regularity establishes a sense of familiarity on the part of the reader, thus strengthening the lines of communication between artist and audience.

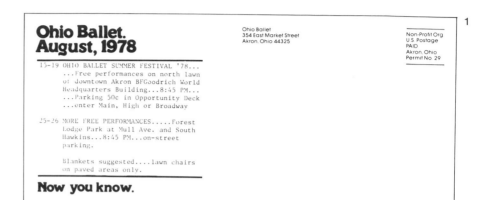

1

**Ohio Ballet.
August, 1978**

15-19 OHIO BALLET SUMMER FESTIVAL '78...
...Free performances on north lawn
of downtown Akron BFGoodrich World
Headquarters Building...8:45 PM...
...Parking 50c in Opportunity Deck
...enter Main, High or Broadway

25-26 MORE FREE PERFORMANCES.....Forest
Lodge Park at Mull Ave. and South
Hawkins...8:45 PM...on-street
parking.

Blankets suggested....lawn chairs
on paved areas only.

Now you know.

Ohio Ballet
354 East Market Street
Akron, Ohio 44325

Non-Profit Org
U.S. Postage
PAID
Akron, Ohio
Permit No. 29

CHILDE BYRON

**William Hurt
in New York Premiere**

Marshall W. Mason will direct William Hurt in the title role of Lord Byron in Romulus Linney's *CHILDE BYRON*, to be performed at the Rep February 18th through March 22nd. The rest of the cast will be announced shortly. *CHILDE BYRON* replaces the previously announced *ANGELO'S WEDDING* as the fourth play of the current season.

In *CHILDE BYRON*, Countess Augusta Ada, Byron's daughter, conjures up the spirit of her father while she lies dying at the age of 36. In a drug induced, emotionally wrenching meeting, father and daughter battle to define their relationship and to discover the truth behind their respective legends.

Historically, Byron never met Ada, for following a notorious scandal when the child was 4 months old, he was separated from his wife and forbidden to see his daughter. He left England and died in Greece at the age, ironically, of 36.

Ada, the brilliant, analytical, detached mathematician who explains in the play the principles of a "thinking machine" that predates the computer by a century, makes a superb foil for the image of Lord Byron, whose impossibly violent, outrageous and intellectually dazzling life was marked by scandals involving incest, rape and bisexuality. Gradually, through a dialogue replete with rich language and compelling images, a portrait of the human spirit emerges.

Romulus Linney was introduced to the world of Byron when he was ejected from his seventh grade class in Madison, Tennessee

William Hurt

and made to read Byron's "The Prisoner of Chillon" as "a kind of punishment."

"I was stunned by it," says Linney, "I had never encountered such sensitivity. I had found my religion."

Linney's plays include a drama about Frederic the Great of Prussia, *THE SORROWS OF FREDERIC, DEMOCRACY, HOLY GHOSTS, OLD MAN JOSEPH AND HIS FAMILY* and *TENNESSEE*, which won him an Obie Award and will appear in the *Best Short Plays of 1980*. His novels include *Heathen Valley, Slowly, By the Hand Unfurled*, and the forthcoming *Jesus Tales*. He has served on the National Endowment for the Arts Literary Panel and has been a visiting professor at many major universities.

Mr. Linney is in the unusual position of having two of his plays produced in New York at the same time. Just before *CHILDE BYRON* opens at the Rep, *THE CAPTIVITY OF PIXIE SHEDMAN* opens at the Phoenix Theatre directed by John Pasquin. There is certain to be marked interest in both productions.

Romulus Linney, author of CHILDE BYRON

William Hurt returns to the Rep at a time when he stars in two major films, Ken Russell's "Altered States" and the forthcoming Peter Yates/Steve Tesich film "Eyewitness" with Sigourney Weaver and Christopher Plummer. Mr. Hurt's distinguished career with the Company is marked by memorable appearances in Milan Stitt's *THE RUNNER STUMBLES* and as Hamlet and Davison in last season's repertory presentations of *HAMLET* and *MARY STUART*. His awards include an Obie for Corinne Jacker's *MY LIFE* and a Theatre World Award for his work during the entire 1977-78 Circle Rep season.

CHILDE BYRON was commissioned by the Virginia Museum Theatre in 1977 and was produced last season by the Actor's Theatre of Louisville. This production marks its New York Premiere.

Ye Waverly Inn 16 Bank Street, 929-4377 Show subscriber card and get 20% off Late Night Supper. Fri.-Sat. only; after 10 p.m.

RITA GARDNER

Say It with Music

Rita Gardner, whose creation of "The Girl" in the original production of *THE FANTASTICKS* is indelibly etched upon the memory of a generation of theatre-goers will give three special concerts at the Rep for friends and subscribers, February 21st, 23rd and March 2nd.

"Say it with Music" is a look at the Twenties as seen through the songs of Rodgers and Hart, Irving Berlin, the Gershwins, Cole Porter, Vincent Youmans, Jerome Kern, Noel Coward and Brecht and Weill, together

with "a few snatches of dialogue" from Scott Fitzgerald and Dorothy Parker. The evening begins with a young girl's coming out party just after World War I and traces her life through the fascinating new rhythms, dances, torch songs and blues of the Twenties until the "lost generation's" ultimate crash in 1929.

Miss Gardner's songs will include Rodgers and Hart's "My Heart Stood Still," and George Gershwin's "The Man I Love," "Little Jazz Bird," and "Innocent Ingenue Baby."

The evening is directed by Will Holt, who wrote the book and/or lyrics for *OVER HERE, ME AND BESSIE*, and the award winning *THE ME NOBODY KNOWS*. Miss Gardner's pianist will be Buddy Barnes, who accompanied Mabel Mercer for many years.

Ticket prices are $4.50 for subscribers and $6.50 for non-subscribers. *Please read the ordering instructions for this event on the next page carefully. Ticket orders will be filled on a first-received basis.*

Rita Gardner

1
_____

Ohio Ballet
Design Firm: Palmer Communications
Creative Director: Craig Palmer

2
_____

Circle Repertory Company
Format: Susan Frank
Design: Marvin Beck
Design Firm: Communigraphics

Photography

In her influential book, *On Photography*, Susan Sontag notes that "Photographs furnish evidence. Something we hear about, but doubt, seems proven when we're shown a photograph of it."

In the performing arts, good photography is essential for precisely this reason. It stands to reason that if photography is indeed our culture's most potent source of visual validation, bad photography has the negative potential for invalidating a performing group's public image.

Unfortunately, photography is one of the most generally neglected areas in the performing arts. Rare is the photographer who can capture that essential moment or gesture or mood on stage and still meet the often restrictive demands of newspaper editors and others. Many press representatives complain that newspaper editors want "only" bad photography—garish, obvious, overlit mug shots. To some extent, this has been true. But it is also true that we are in the midst of a revolution in print communications, in which the general availability of high-quality offset reproduction allows editors much greater freedom in the selection of photographic material. Editors are becoming more sophisticated visually and more at ease with the presence of strong graphics. Newspapers in virtually every major city are experimenting with handsomely-designed entertainment supplements, and the proliferation of city and regional magazines, often with a strong cultural bent, is likely to further extend this trend. In short, there are more outlets for good photography than ever before.

Good photography is a good investment. Beyond the day-to-day publicity applications, there are always the unforeseen needs—a retrospective publication or display, the photo request from a corporate benefactor for its annual report, and so on. Furthermore, as a simple historical record photographic archives are unparalleled. It should be remembered that routine publicity photos rarely record the achievements of set and costume designers who contribute a major part of the total artistic achievement; these elements are captured only in the photographing of actual performance.

Obviously, photography cuts across all the areas we have discussed—posters, illustration, display advertising, fund-raising and direct mail materials, as well as publications. As Sontag has observed, photography is everywhere, touching every aspect of our lives and deeply transforming our perceptions of reality. Performing artists also touch us deeply, and have a responsibility to creatively utilize photography's potential to extend the meaning and impact of their art.

1
The Independent Eye
Macbeth
Photo: Conrad Bishop

One of the busiest cameramen in nonprofit theatre today is New York-based Gerry Goodstein, who has probably frozen on film more resident theatre productions than any other photographer. Goodstein's working approach combines the shooting of nonstop dress rehearsals with carefully-controlled set-ups in which difficult moments can be restaged and/or special publicity shots be created. Like most theatre photographers, however, he considers the recording of actual performance—shot spontaneously with fast lenses and fast film—to be the cornerstone of his craft.

His working arrangements vary from institution to institution. Some companies prefer a minimum of movement on the photographer's part, so as not to distract the actors, but some of Goodstein's most impressive work has been accomplished when (at the director's insistence) he actually moves *onstage* with his cameras, capturing images at close quarters and from unusual perspectives. The technique is not, of course, universally applicable, and is workable only in intimate theatres with closely knit companies. During dress rehearsals at New York's CSC Repertory, for instance, Goodstein is considered a virtual member of the acting en-

Gerry Goodstein

semble. His own prior experience as a professional actor has also given him an invaluable sensitivity to performers dealing with the pressures of final rehearsals.

"There are basic matters of etiquette to be considered," says Goodstein, "like not blocking entrances and exits while shooting—especially a problem in thrust and arena settings, where actors often move in the aisles. Actors should always be introduced to the photographer beforehand. They have a right to know just who that *is* out there, clicking away."

Among the difficulties Goodstein sometimes encounters are "inexperienced actors who don't *complete* their actions on stage, and therefore can be difficult to photograph effectively. The photographer, after all, is waiting for the telling gesture, and must be able to anticipate the timing and the follow-through. Decisive moments are much easier to capture in classical productions, which are usually more broadly played."

In selecting scenes for setups, Goodstein cautions directors and publicists to distinguish between "*important* moments in the play and *visual* moments in the play, because they're often not the same thing." He prefers to have actors speak lines or improvise during setups to avoid overly posed or stiff looking results.

For theatres outside the New York area looking for photographic talent, Goodstein recommends trying "news photographers and photojournalists—people used to working quickly and 'on the spot.' Many otherwise excellent studio photographers are very uncomfortable shooting live performances. Although it may sound funny at first, an experienced *sports* photographer might be the best bet of all."

Goodstein is also a particularly avid baseball fan.

1

2

3

KIRSTEN BECK

KIRSTEN BECK

Photographer: Gerry Goodstein

1
_____
CSC Repertory
Hedda Gabler
Performers: (l-r) Pilar Garcia and Karen Sunde

2
_____
Hartman Theatre Company
Absurd Person Singular
Performers: (l-r) Margot Tenney and Aida Berlin

3
_____
Yale Repertory Theatre
Measure for Measure
Performers: Christopher Walken and Frances Conroy

3

Photographer: Gerry Goodstein

1–3

Circle Repertory Company
Talley's Folly
Performers: Judd Hirsch and
Trish Hawkins

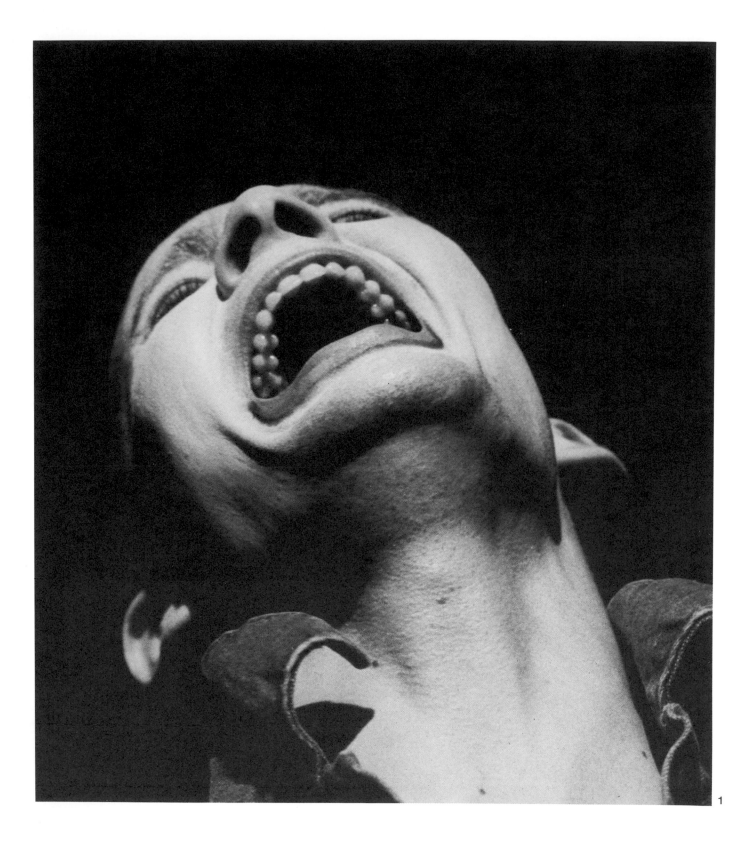

1

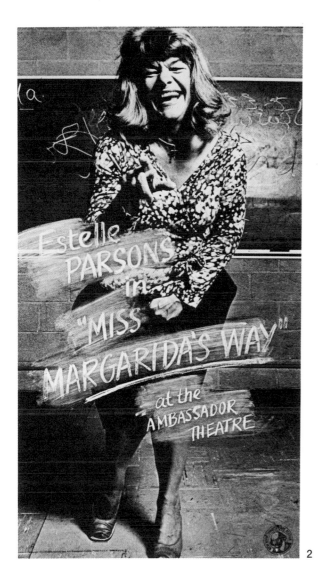

2

1

Arena Stage
Comedians
Photographer: George de Vincent
Performer: Andrew Davis

2

New York Shakespeare Festival
Poster for *Miss Margarida's Way*
Photographer: Jean-Marie Guyaux
Performer: Estelle Parsons
Art Director: Reinhold Schwenk
Agency: Case & McGrath Inc.

3

New Jersey Shakespeare Festival
Annual Report
Photograph: John Cooper
Designer: Jane Cullen
Design Firm: Ciba-Geigy

3

Photography

1

2

3

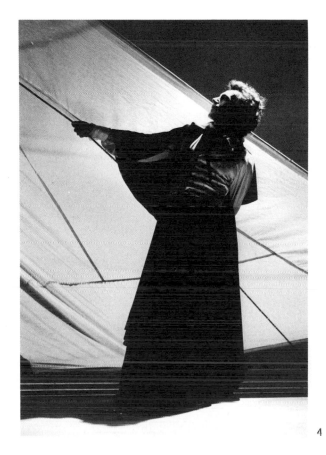

4

"Hedda Gabler"
    Henrik Ibsen

Dir - Lloyd Richards

Influence - Munch -

Hand
Script

← grey
Blank

Z "Hollow" expressions (eyes)

Flames (from poster?)

20"

1. investor
2. his wife
3. judge Brack
4. former lover

D.D. {

colors mix:
6 oz Rhod. Red
10 oz warm "
White
ruffle
1 P1 ↑
Red over Blk
D.O. all type

30"

(Pastel)

Working with a Designer

A good working relationship between an arts institution and its graphic designer is crucial to the successful execution of design projects, but it is an interface which often eludes discussion or analysis, to the detriment of the finished product.

As noted earlier, the artistic, expressive nature of the performing arts makes it a potentially satisfying field for the graphic designer, offering as it does such a visual abundance of raw material. Frustration can result, however, from the occasional clash of creative sensibilities —far more likely in the performing arts arena than, for instance, in the realms of insurance or finance.

Other problems may arise when designers must contend with too many levels of approval (i.e., "design by committee"), vague or poorly defined goals, or insufficient involvement in the conceptual/planning stages of the piece or campaign.

All too often, designers are called upon so late in the life of a project that they can do little more than apply a cosmetic veneer to an ill-conceived communications concept. It cannot be too strongly emphasized that in the area of communications graphics the presentation must never be separated from the intended message. In the most successful projects, they are inevitably developed in tandem.

Professional designers run the gamut from the brilliant to the inept, but the best are communicators and problem solvers. Especially outside the larger metropolitan areas, where designers, design firms and advertising agencies are not likely to have a good deal of experience in the performing arts, designers should be selected with care. When examining a potential designer's portfolio, the client would do well to look for specific qualities.

Is the portfolio simply "flashy" or does it give a real sense of the designer's ability to solve problems? Does the portfolio reflect the work of a designer skilled in creating graphic messages, or the more personal style of a painter or illustrator? The latter might be an ideal choice for a display poster, but a disastrous choice for a subscription brochure.

Cost-conscious institutions should be aware that a large fee in no way guarantees a successful project. One must bear in mind also that larger design firms and agencies inevitably pass along their overhead and payroll expenses to their clients. Shrewd design professionals often keep their capitalization low, and engage support services and personnel only as needed. In the area of fees and contracts, the best resource is the Graphic Artists Guild's *Pricing and Ethical Guidelines* (see "Suggested Reading and Resources").

It is important to view graphic design expenses in terms of a larger financial context. It would not be unreasonable, for example, for an institution that has budgeted $50,000 for the printing and mailing of a subscription brochure to allocate five percent of that expenditure to the design of the piece.

An emerging cost-saving strategy is the sharing of a design or promotional concept by institutions in widely separated geographical areas. The Hartford Stage Company's "Laugh. Cry. Love." campaign, designed by William Wondriska, was effectively utilized by Actors Theatre of Louisville, and later redesigned by the Indiana Repertory Theatre. Care must be taken to select only designs which are appropriate to the adoptive institution, and of course the original designer and institution must be properly credited and compensated for all subsequent uses.

Aspiring designers eager to build their portfolios can often be found in professional design programs, and a good creative director would be wise to contact career development offices at such schools to develop ongoing cooperative programs. Obviously, a student does not have as much time available as a self-employed professional, and does not have the depth of experience to qualify him or her for every project. But the motivated pre-professional can often inject a distinct freshness of vision into even a lackluster assignment.

One institution that has traditionally emphasized communications graphics, both in its professional work and as an integral part of its training for students, is the Yale Repertory Theatre. Lloyd Richards, artistic director of the theatre, and Dean of the Yale School of Drama as well, recently discussed his institution's rare sensitivity and care for its graphic representation:

"When the Yale Rep begins designing an image for a particular production, a series of meetings takes place with our designer, Bob Callahan. At our initial meeting we attempt to illuminate particular concepts for the production which might lend themselves to graphic illustration. Bob generally arrives at that first meeting having read the script of the play, with some preliminary ideas already sketched.

"We try to evaluate those designs and prepare for the next meeting by arriving at a concrete design idea. In the case of Athol Fugard's *Boesman and Lena* Bob and I talked about the *kinds* of people the two main characters were, as well as the environment in which they existed. We were dealing with haunted, hollow creatures living on the sun-bleached mud flats of the Swartkops River in South Africa. Bob came back with images of figures modeled after the drawings of Giacometti—almost abstract stick-figures—walking into an uncertain sunset.

"The image fit the play beautifully, was developed in thumbnail sketches, while placement of all necessary printed material on the poster was determined. The image was transferred effectively into the poster for the show, and adapted for us in our newsletter, program, ads and banners for the front of the theatre.

"In the case of *Hedda Gabler* (as with most of our classical plays) the answers to our design questions were not so clear-cut. Bob came into our earliest meeting with some fascinating ideas, including one which developed the concept of Hedda burning Eilert Lovborg's manuscript. Bob adapted this idea into a photograph of a poster with the words 'Hedda Gabler' on fire. We talked also about my fascination with the work of the artist Edvard Munch—particularly his painting of a woman trapped in a dark forest, and his self-portrait.

"Bob began to develop these two

1–5
Yale Repertory Theatre
Sketches and finished posters
Designer: Robert E. Callahan

146

MARGARET GLOVER

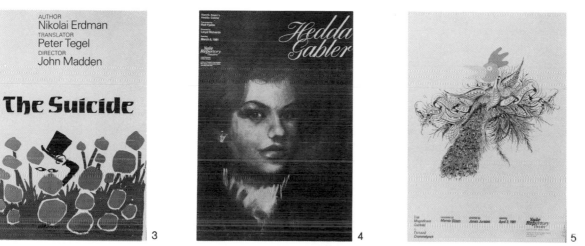

ideas. He also spent an hour in rehearsal, watching our Hedda, Dianne Wiest. And he sketched. He studied Dianne's every move, and left with an indelible image of her in his mind. The Munch self-portrait that we had started with turned into Bob's impression of Dianne Wiest as Hedda Gabler.

"The basic 'feel' of Hedda Gabler was transferred to our banners and programs. It remains, along with the poster for the show, as one of the most stunning graphic interpretations of a play that I have ever seen. And better still, the public made that critical connection between the graphic art which represented the play and the production which they saw on stage. It was a perfect example of a theatre being able, through the use of well coordinated graphic images, to influence an audience's perception of a theatre.

"I believe that the theatre is not doing its job unless it speaks to *all* members of a community—cutting across economic barriers and ethnic types—and puts across this message: something is going on in this theatre that concerns *you*. Graphic design helps send that message out. There are, after all, many ways for the public to view a theatre. They perceive your identity in the things you do both consciously and unconsciously. The unconscious elements—the way the theatre building looks, the appearance of the lobby—mix with the conscious message transferred through brochures, publications, poster art, production photographs, banners and mounted displays in front of the theatre. All elements combine to give the general public—potential patrons of the theatre—some attitude about who you are and what they will see if they walk through your doors.

"At the Yale Rep, close communication between artistic director and graphic designer is critical to a successful image for a contemporary theatre keeping pace with the world."

Designer Callahan at work

MARGARET GLOVER

1, 2
Yale Repertory Theatre
Preliminary renderings and finished
poster for *Boesman and Lena*
Designer: Robert E. Callahan

There are more excellent design publications available today than ever before. In an effort to guide the nonprofit arts institution to those resources of special interest, we offer the following select reading list.

Publications

Graphic Design for Non-Profit Organizations

Peter Laundy and
Massimo Vignelli

This landmark volume is specifically intended to promote coordination, consistency, efficiency and economy in the printed materials of nonprofit institutions. Full graphic systems are devised for two hypothetical organizations, with detailed discussions of formats, grids, typography, logos, symbols and so on. Clearly organized and enormously accessible even to the nondesigner, *Graphic Design for Non-Profit Organizations* is a major step towards enhancing institutional design awareness, and should be considered essential reading. $8.00 plus $.75 postage. American Institute of Graphic Arts, 1059 Third Avenue, New York, NY 10021.

By Design: A Graphics Sourcebook of Materials, Equipment and Services

John Goodchild and Bill Henkin

In many ways the "Whole Earth Catalogue" of the graphic design field, *By Design* features 250 illustrated, information-packed pages covering everything from the comparative quality of marking pens to advice on good business practice. Anyone professionally involved with the production and design of printed communications will find *By Design* a useful and informative

resource. $12.95. Quick Fox Publishers, 33 West 60th Street, New York, NY 10023.

The Art of the Broadway Poster

Michael Patrick Hearn

The history of the American theatrical poster is chronicled in this recent "coffee table" book, most notable for its excellent introductory essay on the forces and fashions that have shaped the direction of this most traditional form of performing arts graphics. $10.95. Ballantine Books, 201 East 50th Street, New York, NY 10022. Available in most bookstores.

Graphic Design USA: 1

American Institute of Graphic Arts

Representing the highest standards in American design, AIGA's *Graphic Design USA* contains over 500 winning entries from its annual competitive exhibitions, and is perhaps the most ambitious and comprehensive annual of its type. A major publishing event. $40. American Institute of Graphic Arts, 1059 Third Avenue, New York, NY 10021.

Communication Arts

One of America's leading graphic design journals, *Communication Arts* provides an excellent means of keeping up-to-date on current trends in advertising, typography, packaging, illustration and photography. Regularly included are portfolio spreads and in-depth interviews with the most innovative designers and design firms in

America. One year subscription: $33. *Communication Arts*, Box 10300, Palo Alto, CA 94303.

Upper and Lower Case

The absolute state-of-the-art in typography and typesetting technology can be found in *Upper and Lower Case*, an attractive, tabloid-sized periodical published quarterly by the International Typeface Corporation. The expressive possibilities of the printed word are probably celebrated nowhere else as they are here; and best of all, this extraordinary publication is available free to communications professionals. *Upper and Lower Case*, 216 East 45th Street, New York, NY 10017.

Pricing and Ethical Guidelines

The Graphic Artists Guild

Essential information on professional standards in matters of contracts, purchase orders, copyright and fair business practice are put forth in *Pricing and Ethical Guidelines*. As we went to press, the third edition was out of print, but the fourth was in preparation and due for 1981 publication. The Graphic Artists Guild, 30 East 20th Street, New York, NY 10003.

Designing with Type: A Basic Course in Typography

James Craig

A widely-used survey of the basic principles of modern typographical design, *Designing with Type* will help demystify the process of specifying type for professional results. Included are suggested exercises and sample assignments for the novice designer. $15. Watson-Guptill Publications, 2160 Patterson Street, Cincinnati, OH 45214.

Production for the Graphic Designer

James Craig

A comprehensive survey of print production: typesetting, printing, paper, inks, binding, folding, imposition and preparation of mechanicals, *Production for the Graphic Designer* is an unusually useful one-volume resource. In addition to an overview of comparative typesetting systems, an extensive glossary of printing terms is included. $19.95. Watson-Guptill Publications, 2160 Patterson Street, Cincinnati, OH 45214.

Layout

Allen Hurlburt

Another influential text, *Layout* provides a basic course in modern design principles with particular emphasis given to the structure of the printed page. Essential reading for all beginners in the design field. $17.95. Watson-Guptill Publications, 2160 Patterson Street, Cincinnati, OH 45214.

Graphic Ideas Notebook

Jan V. White

An extremely useful book, featuring over 1000 techniques for transforming humdrum "raw material" into striking, attention-getting designs. Particular attention is paid to creative use of "found" material and public-domain visuals, especially valuable for small-budget projects and organizations. $14.50. Watson-Guptill Publications, 2160 Patterson Street, Cincinnati, OH 45214.

Get Me to the Printer on Time, on or Under Budget, and Looking Good

Mindy N. Levine and Susan Frank

Still in preparation as we went to press, *Get Me to the Printer...* is aimed specifically at the small non-profit performing group, and will be published by the Off-Off Broadway Alliance, the New York-based service organization. A basic handbook of design procedures and printing processes, it is intended to demystify graphic systems for the uninitiated, and to help groups of all sizes achieve professional results economically and efficiently. Publication date: Summer, 1981. Price not set. For information, contact OOBA, 162 West 56th Street, New York, NY 10019.

While not directly concerned with graphic design, the following publications from TCG can also be of use to the designer seeking information on performing arts institutions, their artistic concerns and practical needs:

Subscribe Now!

Danny Newman

A milestone volume, this best-selling manual on the basic techniques of selling subscription tickets to cultural events can provide the graphic designer with a nuts-and-bolts knowledge of the theories underlying successful audience development campaigns. Devotes major coverage to the preparation of direct mail brochures. $12.95 cloth, $7.95 paper.

Theatre Profiles 4

David J. Skal and Michael Finnegan, Editors

The latest edition of TCG's biennial reference guide to nearly 175 theatres nationwide, *Theatre Profiles 4* is a comprehensive roadmap of institutional theatre, featuring essential information on artistic policy, finances and production history, as well as a range and variety of performance photography unparalleled in print. $12.95.

Both books can be ordered directly from the Publications Department, Theatre Communications Group, Inc., 355 Lexington Avenue, New York, NY 10017. A complete publications catalog will be included with each order.

Service Organizations

In addition to TCG's wide-ranging informational services, the following organizations can also be helpful in providing useful background material on specific artistic disciplines:

Off-Off Broadway Alliance (OOBA)
162 West 56th Street, Suite 206
New York, NY 10019
(212) 757-4473

American Symphony Orchestra League
Post Office Box 669
Vienna, VA 22180
(703) 281-1230

National Association for Regional Ballet
1860 Broadway
New York, NY 10023
(212) 757-8460

Opera America
1010 Vermont Avenue SW,
Suite 702
Washington, DC 20005
(202) 347-9262

ALAN KRAUSS

About the Editor

David J. Skal, publications director
for Theatre Communications
Group since 1978, has an extensive
background in nonprofit theatre,
and has developed promotional
campaigns and materials for major
arts groups from Connecticut to
California, including the Hartford
Stage Company and the American
Conservatory Theatre in San Francisco. A graduate of Ohio University, Athens, he received training in
arts management as a public affairs
intern at the National Endowment
for the Arts. In addition to his work
in theatre and graphics, Mr. Skal is
the author of two provocative
novels, *Scavengers* and *When We Were
Good*. He makes his home in New
York's Greenwich Village.

About the Designer

Robert E. Callahan is currently a
design director at the communications firm of Ted Colangelo Associates in White Plains, New York. A
graduate of New York's School of
Visual Arts, where he studied under Bob Gill, Milton Glaser and
others, he headed his own design
office, Design Collaborative, in Old
Greenwich, Connecticut, from 1967
to 1979. In addition to his work on
corporate accounts, Mr. Callahan
has designed graphics for a number
of performing arts organizations,
including the Yale Repertory Theatre in New Haven and the Hartman Theatre Company in Stamford, as well as publications for
Theatre Communications Group.
He lives with his wife, six children
and numerous pets in Stamford,
Connecticut.